# Growing Up in Stearns County

Richard W. Job

# Contents

# Introduction

This book is a series of snippets from the children of Ralph and Wilhelmina Job about growing up as they remember. It is not necessarily a true historical dialogue. Many of these recollections are just that and may not all be entirely factual. I apologize for the quality of the pictures, but they almost all came from Grandma Job's album and date back to the times shown. The color pictures are ones I took shortly before I left home for college; they show I am not a great photographer. I've done my best to capture the memories and what we know about our family. I hope you add your own stories over time.

# Chapter 1

# Andreas Job and Settling the Farm

*Andreas Job*

Andreas Job emigrated from Germany in 1861. We believe he served in the Prussian army for at least one enlistment. His mother had died, and his father had remarried while Andreas was in the army. He and his stepmother did not get along. She was "Auch de kritisch mutter!"—roughly translated as "the critical mother."

Andreas got as far as Madison, Wisconsin, before he ran out of money. The Civil War was going on—if he served at least one enlistment, he was entitled to a 160-acre homestead in exchange for his service. He enlisted in a regiment and served two enlistment terms. He was wounded in the Siege of Petersburg in 1865 and was hospitalized for several months. According to legend, when he was injured, they did not find him at the end of the day. He collected several muskets to protect himself from body robbers who always came to the battlefields at night. Early the next morning, three such persons did come. He shot two of the robbers, but the third one was quick on his feet and got away.

When Andreas did not show up for roll call that morning, they listed him as AWOL; he has later confirmed to be in the hospital. He was hospitalized in Germantown, Pennsylvania, north of Washington, DC. The surgeon wanted to amputate his leg above the knee, but he begged the surgeon to leave it on. He was mustered out of the army in 1865 after he was discharged from the hospital. Along with Alyois Altman—whom he had met at Ellis Island when they emigrated to the US—and supposedly a man with the last name Kuch—whom they had met while in the army—he traveled to Minnesota to homestead.

In my search to learn Kuch's (Kuck's) first name, I contacted the Stearns History Museum. There is no record of Kuch homesteading. The homestead records indicate that property was homesteaded by Christian Graeser. The records indicate that

Andreas (Andrew on those records), Alyois Altman, and Christian Graeser homesteaded the properties. Those records are all dated in 1871—five years after they had established their homestead. So, if there was a Kuch involved, he had to have left in the first year so that Graeser could establish the homestead.

There were two active German settlements in Minnesota. The one at New Ulm had an Indian raid the year before. Having just come out of the army, Andreas decided to go further north to a new German settlement at New Munich—he had enough of war. There, he settled on a quarter section of land under the Homestead Act. To reduce their labor, he and the other young men built one shack on the intersection of their connecting properties to qualify as a house for all three pieces of land, each sleeping on his own land.

Evidently, because of his disability, Andreas did most of the cooking. One time, he burnt the bread. The three men exchanged many words and got into a heated discussion. They ended up chasing each other around the outside of the cabin until they cooled off. This argument happened in the winter, so it was too cold to fight for very long.

When we were growing up, there was a stone at the northwest corner of the granary with an "X" on one face—that could have been the corner marker. The location of that stone would have aligned with the original property lines as the three settlers platted it. In the ensuing years, each man built his own house and farmstead while clearing the land

and harvesting the crops. The "Kuch" farm became the Buckholz farm and later the Friedel farm. It is now owned by the National Wildlife Federation as a wildlife refuge; the buildings were razed in the 1980s. Alois Altman owned the Altman farm until Dad purchased it in 1950. My brother Eddie and his family have farmed it since.

When Andreas was getting married, Alyois Altman deeded 1.5 acres to Andreas as a wedding present—this land now makes up most of the farmyard. If you stood at the stone with an X near the granary and looked out toward the east road that served as the property line between the Altman farm and Friedel farm, you could get a feel for the one and a half acres cut off from the original farm.

After Buckholz bought the farm to the east, he and Andreas would argue because Andreas's chickens would get into the Buckholz field and eat his grain. The St. Joe–New Munich Road also ran through the land, and the Soo Line Railroad came through in 1906. These property changes left a thin sliver of land—reported to be less than thirty feet wide—and Buckholz could hardly turn his horses around when pulling farm machinery. Buckholz sold that sliver of land to Andreas. This seemed to resolve the chicken issue. Andreas bought forty more acres—that we would come to know as "the woods"—at a government sale in 1866. The "woods" were about a half mile northeast of the buildings and about a quarter mile behind the buildings on the Altman Farm.

102

**The United States of America,**

**TO ALL TO WHOM THESE PRESENTS SHALL COME, GREETING:**

Homestead Certificate No. *623*

Application *1327*

**Whereas,** there has been deposited in the **General Land Office** of the United States, a **CERTIFICATE** of the *Register* of the *Land Office* at *St Cloud Minnesota*, whereby it appears that pursuant to the *Act of Congress* approved 20th May, 1862, "*To secure Homesteads to actual settlers on the public domain,*" and the acts supplemental thereto, the claim of *Alois Altmann*

has been established and duly consummated in conformity to law for the *Lot numbered one, the East half of the North West quarter, and the South West quarter of the North East quarter of section twenty-three, in Township one hundred and twenty five, of Range thirty-two, in the District of Lands subject to sale at St Cloud Minnesota Containing one hundred and sixty one Acres, and twenty five hundredths of an acre, Excess paid as per receipt No 2471.*

according to the Official *Plat* of the *Survey* of the said *Land* returned to the **General Land Office** by the SURVEYOR GENERAL.

**Now know ye,** That there is therefore granted by the UNITED STATES unto the said *Alois Altmann* the tract of Land above described: **To Have and to Hold** the said tract of Land, with the appurtenances thereof, unto the said *Alois Altmann* and to *his* heirs and assigns forever.

**In Testimony whereof,** I, *Ulysses S. Grant*, PRESIDENT OF THE UNITED STATES OF AMERICA, have caused these letters to be made *Patent*, and the **Seal of the General Land Office** to be hereunto affixed.

*Given* under my hand, at the CITY OF WASHINGTON, the *eighteenth* day of *August*, in the year of *Our Lord* one thousand eight hundred and *seventy one*, and of the *Independence of the United States* the *Ninety Sixth*.

*By the President:* *U. S. Grant*

*By* *J. Parrish*, Sec'y.

*C B Boynton*, Recorder of the General Land Office.

**Andreas's homestead document**

# Chapter 2

# Andreas Job and Family

After settling on the farm, Andreas met and married Anna Sperl. They had four children, but Anna died in childbirth on January 23, 1875. The baby died three days later. The other children died of diphtheria in 1876.

| Andreas Job | 1831 – 1922 |
| Anna Sperl Job | 1847 – 1875 (Married 1866 or 1867) |
| Many | 1870 – 1876 |
| Ottlilig | 1872 – 1876 |
| Joseph | 1873 – 1876 |
| Andreas | 1875 – 1875 |

Andreas then married Julie Sura, and they had eight children—one of whom only lived a few hours.

***Julie Sura Job***

| | |
|---|---|
| Julie Sura Job | 1851 - 1922 (Married in 1877) |
| Joseph | 1877 - 1894 (Died of an epileptic seizure) |
| Lewis | 1878 - 1956 |
| George | 1879 - 1957 |
| Katie | 1880 - 1971 |
| Margaret | 1883 - 1942/44 |
| Henry | 1885 - 1941 |
| Conrad | 1888 - 1970 |
| Anthony | 1890 - 1890 |

**In the old country, Andreas was evidently a chauffeur or groomsman because he was very good**

with horses. His horses always got good treatment and a proper diet and served him well. The yard was fenced, and the horses were allowed to graze in the yard at night. It also made getting the horses ready the next day easier.

Andreas was a good wine maker—he built a special stone house for his winery/wine cellar. We knew it as the smoke house just east of the big house. At various times, he shared the wine with his friends and neighbors. The neighbors began to tease him that they would come over sometime when he was gone and help themselves. Andreas's reply was, "I have a good watchdog." The neighbors collaborated to play a joke on him and visited his winery one evening when Andreas was gone. To get past the watch dog, they brought along a bitch in heat. They helped themselves to some wine and let Andreas know they were able to do so.

The young people used to carry a pistol in their pocket when they walked to town to ward off wild animals. There was also some horseback travel as there are pictures of family members riding saddled horses.

Andreas' sons George and Henry left New Munich and moved to Mt. Clemons, North Dakota, in reply to a newspaper ad to work a farm there. They were there for twelve years, after which George returned unannounced, and he would not talk about his time there. Several years later, someone from that North Dakota area visited. In the conversations, the visitor revealed that George and Henry had been sweet on the same lady. They got into a fight over her, and George left. As far as we know, Henry did not marry the lady either. Henry reportedly moved on to Great Falls, Montana. Records indicate that he died there.

George was back at the farm in 1917 and helped build the new house. Sometime after that, he moved to California and bought a farm and orange grove in Pomona. My grandpa Lewis and his wife Elizabeth stayed with George after they left the farm. George was still farming into the 1950s. Grandpa was a very successful farmer and, at one time, owned another farm north of Melrose. After George passed away, Uncle Louis sold the farm in Pomona to developers, and it is now a housing development.

One time after Andreas had retired and moved to Melrose, he came back to visit the farm. Lewis, my grandpa, didn't know how Andreas would react to the new tractor Lewis had bought, so he hid the tractor behind the granary across the railroad tracks during Andreas's visit. There is not much more information about this family growing up; that seems to have been lost as the older generation died.

As he got older Andreas began to have difficulty walking due to his war injury. In the last several years, he was pretty much confined to a wheelchair. I can remember an early-era wheel chair in our attic; it was removed sometime in my younger years, as I couldn't find it later on.

# Chapter 3

# Grandparents Lewis Job and Elizabeth (Hagen)

*Nettie Ndoskey, Jospeph Singer, Elizabeth (Hagen) Job, and Lewis Job*

L ewis and Lizzie had two biological children:

Ralph     April 14, 1908 – January 21, 1998
Louis     August 1909 – 1961

*Louis and Ralph*

In 1909 or 1910, Elizabeth had an appendicitis attack. By the time they got her to the hospital in St. Cloud, it had ruptured. She survived, but she could not have any more children. They then adopted:

Mary (Mrs. Tony Rhu)
Martha (Mrs. Dominic Finneman)

Grandpa's sister Margaret lived with them. She was burned in an incident when she was young—between six and nine years old. She was cleaning up shavings from a cabinet that was being built in the basement. She put the shavings into her apron, and when she threw them into the fire, the fire flared up onto her apron and severely burned her. The burns and pain affected her mind, and she never developed mentally as an adult. Margaret continued to live on the farm until about the time Ralph and Minnie were married. Around 1930, she moved to a convent in Melrose and later moved to their mother's house in Fergus Falls, MN, where she died in 1942.

Grandpa and Grandma kept cats in their house to keep the mouse population at bay. One day, when Dad or Uncle Louis was a baby—I'm not sure who—Grandpa went to the crib to pick up the baby but found the tomcat sitting in the crib staring at the baby. The tomcat went flying out the door and was not allowed in the house again.

Grandpa developed his own version of hybrid corn. While hunting every year, he would visit some farms around the area and pick a few good ears to mix with his seed corn. He stowed the ears in his hunting jacket—which had room for birds he shot. He generally had a better than average corn crop.

Once when Grandpa was cutting grain with the binder, the seat broke off, and he fell to the ground. Grandma was shocking the grain bundles and happened to see him fall—she laughed very hard. He was upset and sent her all the way back to the farmstead to get a seat from another machine. She did not think it was as funny by the time she got back with the replacement seat.

Grandpa and Grandma loved to tell stories. One of Grandpa's stories was: "If a man lost his toes, he would have difficulty walking, as his toes were a major element in his sense of balance." Grandma told the story about my cousin Kenny in California who ran into the house all excited and said, "Granny, Granny, come quick. There's a possum in the stay hack." Another one of Grandma's stories was about when she was washing clothes and found a ten-dollar bill in the wash. She did not ask if anyone had lost the money, and when no one mentioned that they were missing money, she kept it.

Grandma also told the story about having a "bum" come to the back door asking for food. Keep in mind that the back door of the house was about 200 feet from the railroad tracks. She was obliging until he started getting forceful. She backed further into the house where she had a shotgun. She chased him off with it. She kept it loaded for quite some time after that incident.

*Lewis' hunting dogs and guns*

Grandpa sold the farm and used the proceeds to invest in a "sure thing." The sure thing turned out to be a scam, and he lost the money. The contact they worked through went to jail, but he no longer had any of their money, so they didn't get it back.

Grandma used to cook all the meals in the basement and bring them upstairs to serve, which seemed like a lot of extra work. I suppose it worked well in the summer, as it would have been cooler to cook downstairs. But it was a lot of work to bring the food upstairs to eat. When I was young, I wondered at times why there was a cook stove downstairs. Grandma told my sister Clara that she fell down those basement steps when she was in her 30's. After that incident, she started having joint pains, which were later diagnosed as arthritis.

In my younger years, Grandpa and Grandma Job spent the winters in California and the summers with us in Minnesota. I always looked forward to them coming in late May or early June. They usually returned to California in September before the mountain passes would close due to snow.

Grandpa had been sick in California through most of 1948 and 1949. He was diagnosed with colon cancer in 1949 and had abdominal surgery for it. The doctor gave him six months to live. He and Grandma decided that if he was going to die, he wanted to be in Minnesota and be buried in New Munich.

In 1950, Dad flew out to California—where Grandpa and Grandma were living with George in Pomona—and drove them in their car back to Minnesota. It took four days to drive back in Grandpa's 1938 Pontiac. They moved into the small bedroom next to Mom and Dad's room on the south side of the house. The surgery and the move to Minnesota were evidently successful as he lived six years after they came to Minnesota. Grandpa was very active and lived just short of his 77th birthday in 1956. During the last two years, the cancer returned. The last year was very difficult for him.

The new living situation made for a full house and a difficult arrangement for Ma. I will give Ma and Grandma credit that they made the best of a difficult situation. Ma said much later that they should have found a house in either Freeport or New Munich for them.

When Grandpa came to live with us, he brought a 0.29cc model airplane engine. He tried to get it running but never could. It would usually start but then sputter and eventually stop. This hobby was not successful until Jimmy came and brought the glow plug ignition system (more on that later).

After they came to live with us, Grandma spent most of her time knitting and crocheting. She made doilies and many decorative pieces. She also crocheted fancy handkerchiefs. Each of the girls in the family received a hand-crocheted bedspread from her.

Grandpa loved to fish. After they came to live with us and he got well, we bought a boat, and we built a trailer to tow it to the various lakes in the area. There were many fishing trips to local lakes. Grandpa towed the eighteen-foot wooden Larsen boat with his 1938 Pontiac. Part of the fun was going to the lake while Grandpa drove—it gave us a chance to horse around and see a little of the countryside.

Grandpa loved to cast for Northern Pike while the rest of us fished with cane poles for sunfish or crappies. On one such fishing trip, on Art's backswing, he caught me with the hook just under the left eye. We couldn't pull the hook out backward because of the barb at the end. Grandpa had to cut the skin to remove the hook. Luckily, the hook missed my eye, and there is no scar from that incident.

One year, Grandpa discovered horseradish growing along the fence across the tracks. Since he liked horseradish, he was excited. He had several helpings of it. Late that fall, when he went to harvest more of it, he found the area dug up. Some small hogs had also found it and rooted it all out. He never found any more horseradish.

Grandma told of someone in the early settlement days finding goose eggs. The lady of the house decided to make a special apron which held the eggs next to her body—the warmth would help them hatch. Her plan was successful, and they had geese for several years added to their food supply.

# Chapter 4

# Grandparents Bernard Wensmann and Elizabeth (Hoppe)

*Bernard and Elizabeth (Hoppe) Wensmann*

Bernard Wensmann (1871-1947) married Elizabeth Hoppe (1875- 1949) in Breckenridge, MN on July 3, 1899. They had four children:

| | |
|---|---|
| Wilhelmina (Minnie) | April 10, 1905 – January 25, 1987 |
| Alyouis (Al) | 1909 – 2001 |
| Clara | October 22, 1911-1982 |
| Paul | 1913-2003 |

Grandpa was a big man and carried himself well. Grandma was a tiny woman who always wore gold loop earrings in her pierced ears. They farmed northeast of Freeport until about 1924 when they bought the farm southeast of the Job farm. My ma, Minnie, was eighteen when they moved to that farm. Ma and her parents spoke "Plattdeutsch" when they were together. I can remember understanding only a few words when they spoke.

Grandpa and Grandma retired from the farm when Uncle Al married Aunt Betty. We knew that farm as Uncle Al and Aunt Betty's place. We spent a lot of time with them and their kids. After Grandpa and Grandma retired, they moved to New Munich where Clara purchased a small farmstead on the east side of town. The farm consisted of a house, a small barn with room for horses, a few cows for milk, and a garage (it seems like they drove a model "A" Ford). There were also a few acres of pasture to the east of the barn.

Clara had polio as a child, from six to eight years old, and they spent a lot of time and money on doctor visits and trips to the Mayo Clinic in Rochester.

There were quite a few operations, and she had to take a lot of medicine. She finally said, "No more operations."

She was paralyzed from the chest down and wore a full-body brace and leg braces with special shoes, which formed the lower support for the leg braces. She walked with crutches by lifting herself with her arms and swinging her legs forward; as a result, she had very strong arms. In the 1950s, she said she wore forty pounds of hardware to be able to get around. She did virtually everything she wanted to do, including gardening and driving a car when automatic transmissions became available. She worked at Worms Lumber in New Munich, was a very outgoing person with a very forceful personality, and was probably the favorite of all our family members. She and Ma spent a lot of time visiting, and she always had encouraging words for all of us.

After Grandpa and Grandma Wensmann died, he in 1947 and she in 1949, Clara stayed on in New Munich for several years working for the Worms Lumber Yard. She finally sold the house, moved to St. Paul, and lived with family friends—the Westholders. A few years later, she met E. J. Fitzgerald, a widower, and they were married in 1953. They were favorites to visit for many years. E.J. was the Chief Deputy in the Register of Deeds office and later was elected to the Clerk of Court for Ramsey County until he retired in 1972.

# Chapter 5

# Ralph and Wilhelmina (Wensmann) Job

*Ralph and Wilhelmina (Wensmann) Job*

Ralph and Wilhelmina (Minnie) were married on May 21, 1929 at the Immaculate Conception Church in New Munich. They started farming at Ralph's home farm because Grandpa Lewis and Grandma Elizabeth wanted to travel and spend the winters in California where Grandpa's brother George had a farm with an orange grove. Grandpa had already spent the winter before in California.

**Together, they had eleven children.**

*Dolores (April 29, 1930 – May 2018) Married Roman Waldorf June 23, 1953 (d. 2008?)*

*Dorothy (April 19, 1931 – – – –) Married Jim Blommel September 13, 1956 (d. 2004?)*

*Edward (Eddie) (April 21, 1932 – July 2020) Married*
*Agnes Fleischaker June 6, 1957 (d. 2017)*

*Marcella (Sally) (May 23, 1933 – September 2004)*
*Married Nick Berschied June 29, 1955 (d. 2000)*

*Arthur (Artie) (November 15, 1934 - ---) Married
Joan Urbashich June 7, 1960*

*Louis (Sonny) (July 18, 1936 - ---) Married Matilda
Fleischaker July 7, 1962*

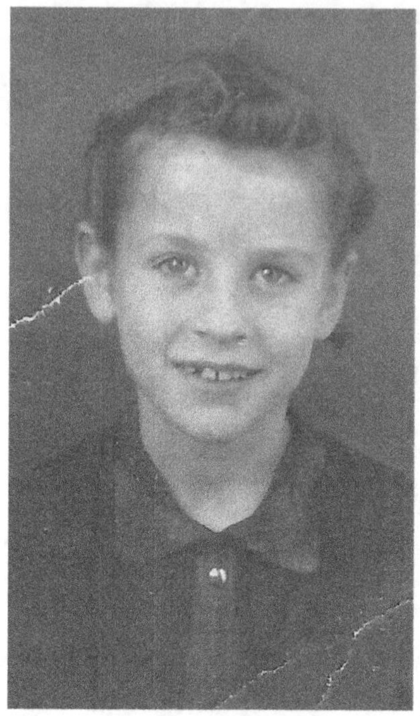

*Mary Jane (August 3, 1937 - ---) Married John Urbashich August 23, 1958 (d. 2017)*

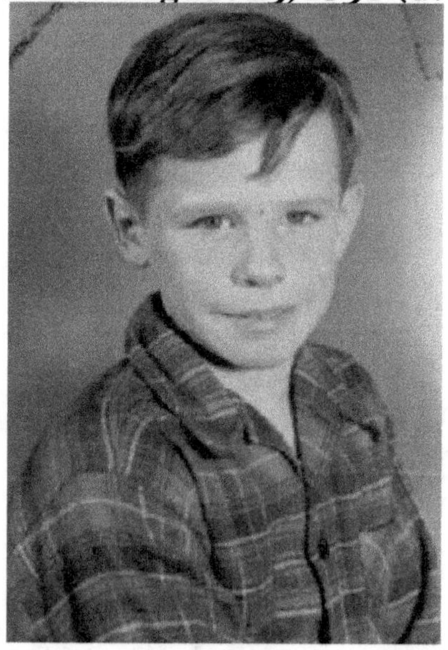

*Harold (October 15, 1938 - October 20, 1956)*

*Richard (Rich) (December 12, 1939 - ---) Married
Jane Friberg May 26, 1962 (d. 2015)*

*Clara (August 15, 1942 - ---) Married Jerry
Michaels May 9, 1964*

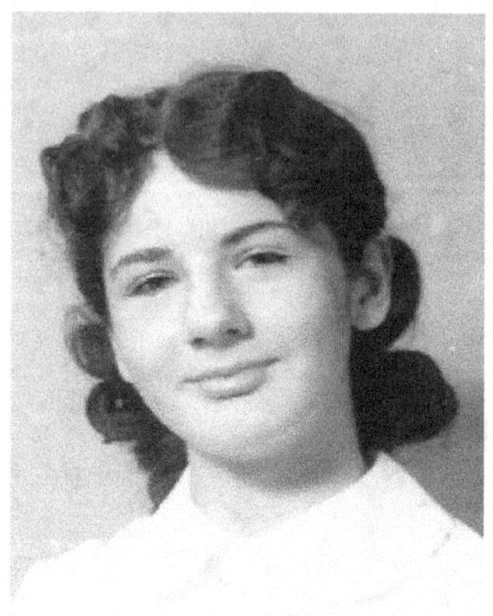

*Ethel (January 21, 1945 - ---) Married Bernard Carlson July 5, 1969 (d. 2020)*

# Home Life

The girls slept in the northeast bedroom; it was the largest and, though crowded, had room for all six of them. The boys had the bedroom between the kitchen and Mom and Dad's bedroom. Eddie moved upstairs when he was in the early teens. Art and Sonny moved upstairs when I was five or six. For some time, only Harold and I shared a bedroom. We moved upstairs when Grandpa and Grandma came to live with us in 1950.

Mattresses were expensive, so we used corn ear husks stuffed into a hand-sewn cover. We changed these out periodically. Later, we all got mattresses for our beds. Sometime before Harold and I moved upstairs, the ceiling on the upstairs bedroom was insulated, which helped keep those rooms warm. The upstairs walls were uninsulated, and those rooms were unheated, so we used a lot of heavy blankets and quilts in the winter. Ma or the church quilting group made most of the quilts. You could feel the cold air coming in around the doors to the attic. When it was really cold, we used a deer hide blanket on top of the other covers. We undressed and got into bed very quickly to warm our blanket cocoon as quickly as possible. When you got up in the morning, there was no lollygagging as you got into your clothes as fast as possible and moved on downstairs.

There were some very severe snowstorms when we were growing up. I can remember missing school for several days while different storms raged. Up to sometime in the mid-1950s, the road from the crossroad west of the farm to Freeport was very low and had trees and brush growing along the side of it. Invariably, the snow would block the road in those areas. One year, when Dad was working in Freeport, he had to drive to New Munich, north to US 52, then back east to get to Freeport because the road was blocked for several days. I remember another time in the late 1940s or early 50s when the man who plowed the roads had to push the grader with the "vee plow" and a truck to get through a particularly deep blockage. On one severe drift, they had to "hit" the drift several times to get through. There were some pictures of a couple of the girls standing on top of the snowbank— the top of the bank was less than two feet below the telephone line on the side of the road.

Mom used to talk about the severe winter of 1939-40. That winter started on Armistice Day, November 11. It had been quite warm, but then the wind came up, the temperature dropped, and it started to snow. Overnight, the storm covered everything with snow. The next morning, when Dad, Dolores, and Eddie went outside to do chores, they came back looking like snowmen as their clothes were covered with snow.

In 1940, some people got stuck in their cars and froze to death. There were also a lot of animals that did not have proper shelter and froze to death. That year, the snow did not melt until late spring. One storm I remember was when Elmo Laing and his family lived in the small second house on the Pfau farm. Elmo would take us to school in the morning on his way to work. After this storm, we didn't have much trouble getting through, but the snow on the road was packed so hard that the car drove over the top of the drifts.

In the wintertime, we would go sledding on the big hill about a quarter-mile to the west of the house. It had at least a thirty-foot vertical drop and a run several hundred feet long. It almost always had snow on the east face. This was a favorite Sunday afternoon winter excursion. We had one big sled that could hold four or five of us and at least one or two single-person sleds. Many times, after coming back to the house and going inside to dry off and warm up, we would have popcorn and something to drink.

For a few years, we had a propeller-driven iceboat. It was a crude, 2x4 wood airplane frame without wings and had a homemade wood propeller on a four-cylinder Wisconsin engine at the front with steel channel runners—the engine came from the baler. We would take it on Overman's lake—approximately two miles southeast of our farm—and get some very fast rides. Dad was the driver.

Ma had buck teeth. It didn't bother us; it was just normal. I do remember on a few occasions that kids at school commented on someone having buck teeth like Minnie Yup. "Yup" is the grammatical pronunciation of our family name in German. We spoke German as a family at home. Our prayers were also in German. Our grace before the meal included an "Our Father" and a "Hail Mary." We said the Angelus with grace after each meal.

We kids did not know English very well when we started school, but it wasn't an issue. Kids typically learn very quickly, so learning English wasn't too hard. In the evenings during the school year, Ma would have us show her our schoolwork, so she knew we were doing our lessons and keeping up in school. I believe we all did well, as I do not remember hearing any criticism of our work.

We usually got new shoes towards fall as we were getting ready for school. We bought the shoes at the "Corner Store." It was a special day because we could see all the shoes available and find one to fit us. The shoes were supposed to last a year, but they usually had to be re-soled to get us through the year. There was a shoe repair shop in Freeport that seemed to do good business judging by the number of shoes and other leather goods there for repair. As the harness repair business fell off, there was not enough business in just shoe repair, and the family who ran the repair shop left Freeport in the early 1950s.

When we started school each fall, we each got a set of school or "good" clothes. One year, my school outfit was a beige shirt with a brown corduroy bib overall. I was quite proud to be wearing such a nice outfit. In the summertime, we went barefoot. Once we were working every day, we had to wear our shoes all the time because we were into too many things that could cause cuts or punctures to bare feet. We always had at least two pairs of work clothes we wore at home.

Dad worked for Freeport Implement from 1938 to 1940. During that time, they switched from their church in New Munich to one in Freeport. Supposedly, Dad asked the parish priest about the cost of having the kids go to school in Freeport, and he replied there would be no cost if they became parishioners. It was more convenient getting the kids to school in Freeport. Dorothy also remembers that it was special to go to Freeport because she learned so much more at that school.

Meals were also a special time. If possible, everyone sat down at the table to eat together. In my younger years, we ate at a long table on the west side of the dining room, with the window seat serving as the boys' chairs. We lined up oldest to youngest, and if you had to leave the table early, you had to get up and walk on the window seat behind those still seated. After Grandpa and Grandma moved in with us in 1950, we moved that table to the center of the dining room. The table was not long enough, so we elongated and strengthened the table and added more leaves. We bought more chairs which gave all of us—fifteen when everyone was there—a place at the table.

When we were sawing logs (which I'll get to later in the book), there were usually extra people around, and they always ate with the family. No matter who it was, if someone had business that required them to be there through the dinner hour, they were fed. One morning, I came up from the barn, and there was a "bum" having breakfast at the back steps. As I remember, he got a very good meal.

I can remember many times racing to the house and getting in line to wash our hands and face—done at the kitchen sink as it was the only wash facility in the house—and getting to our place at the table. We would then say grace before our meal. After the meal, no one could leave the table until we had said grace again unless there was a very special reason for leaving.

When I was quite young, we were saying grace before our meal when I spotted a fly on something on the table. I became so fascinated with it that I forgot all about praying and blurted out "De fliege—" translated "The fly—." Red-faced, I realized we were still praying. Everyone had a good laugh as they concluded the prayer.

Mom liked the marrow in the bones. She would select a piece of meat with a bone in it and eat the marrow from the center of the bone. She also liked to chew the last of the meat off a bone. She was usually the last one finished at meals because she was getting the last of the meat off a bone. After she had her big buck teeth pulled, Dad would sometimes admonish her for still eating the marrow. He thought she would break her partial front teeth.

Sunday meals were extra special. At noon, we usually had soup—either chicken or beef, with a pearl barley soup on occasion. Sometimes, Ma made "pigs in a blanket," which were cabbage leaves with specially prepared pork inside. It was quite good. Our evening meal was usually some type of sausage, a vegetable, and then a special sauce or cake for dessert.

Our meals during lent were interesting because Fridays were meat-free. When there were no fish available, and other non-meat meals had been already served, Ma would make a creamed noodle soup. It wasn't spectacular, but it got us a meat-free meal.

Dad always took a 20-30-minute nap after dinner, our noon meal. It usually gave us kids a chance to horse around. However, Dad's glass eye always seemed to be watching.

In 1947, Dad lost his left eye—he was driving a nail into an oak board when the nail broke off, ricocheted off something, and pierced his eye. He had to go to the hospital. The person in the other bed in the hospital room was Mom's cousin, Joe Hoppe. He had been warming a pan of gasoline to wash parts on a stove when he spilled some. The fire flashed up, burning him quite severely in the hands and face. He worked for us part-time at the sawmill for several years after that.

Dad had to get a glass eye and a pair of glasses. The socket with the prosthetic always oozed a little when he was out in inclement weather; in his later years, he had the lens on the glasses tinted dark, and he would place a cotton ball there to absorb the pus on his face. The thing I remember most was that the eyelid did not close completely, so when he was asleep for his nap, that eye seemed to be looking at you. Even after having lost one eye, he could still see very well. He joked at various times about how hard it was to keep his glasses clean in all the things he did. However, he was very disappointed—because of his eye, the Minnesota aeronautics rules would not let him get his pilot's license. According to their rules, even though he could see well, his depth perception was not good enough. Having only one eye did not stop him from doing any work he wanted to do. He demonstrated to us through his actions that his depth perception was as good as ours. He was involved with building projects and farm work and never let his eye keep him from completing a task.

Dad was a practical joker and loved to tell stories. In the 1950s, he and a friend were converting the sawmill from a wood timber structure to a steel base structure. They were in the shop when a salesman came to sell some tools for the lathe. Dad was working at the lathe, and George was busy doing something close to the door. When the salesman asked for Dad, George acted as though Dad wasn't there. The salesman then walked over to Dad and asked for Ralph. Dad answered that he wasn't there. They were evasive when the salesman pressed for a time of return. The salesman finally left after getting no satisfaction from the two of them.

In his younger adult years, one of Dad's favorite practical jokes was getting close to an idling tractor or other engine and grabbing the closest person and a spark plug wire at the same time—spark plug wires had an exposed end at the connection to the spark plug. Dad, of course, would get a shock, but the other person, not suspecting it, would literally jump from the shock. It got so that Henry, the local implement dealer, would not stand close to Dad if they were near a running engine.

Dad made it quite difficult to take a picture of him for a number of years. Aunt Betty would call out to him and have the camera ready to get a shot when he turned to look. It worked sometimes when she was very quick. Usually, the pictures came out with him covering his face and turning away from the camera.

Dad also had a reputation for being somewhat grouchy and hard-nosed. Mary Jane's husband, Buddy, was a bit nervous when he started dating Mary Jane. Mary Jane was scaling the lumber, and Buddy thought that this was a gal he could work with. Buddy wondered what reaction he would get from Dad when he started to date Mary Jane since Dad had a reputation as being rather gruff. I never heard that Dad objected to Buddy. The only comment I did hear was that if Buddy was like his dad, he would be a hard worker.

He used his determined nature to get good deals on things he needed. He once went to an auction because he needed to replace one set of horse harnesses. He waited until the bidding slowed, and then he got into it. The bidding got down to him and one other person, and every time Dad bid, the other person would raise the bid by a very small amount. After a couple of rounds like that, Dad jumped the bid by two dollars. He got the harness that he needed, and he still paid less than the upper limit he had set for his bid. I believe he paid $32.00 for the harness in the late 1920s.

Dad loved to talk with the merchants and people in town. In the late 1940s or early 1950s, a merchant opened a TV-Electronics store on the north side of town. Several times, we stopped in after school, and Dad would talk to the owner. We kids had a chance to watch a very snowy TV picture while Dad chatted away. Despite working with engines and exhaust noise spending all those years as a sawyer on the sawmill, Dad still had excellent hearing. Even into his eighties, he could still hear as well as I could—possibly better—which made it easy for him to listen to Mom sing.

Mom had a good singing voice. You could hear her sing as she worked. She knew many songs which were popular in her day, as well as many religious songs. The religious songs were not necessarily Catholic Church hymns. She knew many others as well. At the remembrance for her, one of the mourners commented that he heard her singing at mass the morning she died. She also knew many of the contemporary songs of the era and would sing them as she worked. She also knew and sang many German songs. I suppose that is where I got my love for music—I often find myself singing under my breath.

Before we got a console radio-phonograph, we had a wind-up phonograph that stood approximately thirty inches tall and eighteen inches wide. The mechanism was in a box on the upper half of the unit, which had a dark walnut finish. The phonograph arm was massive and swiveled on a centering arm. The playing head swiveled down from the arm so the needle could connect with the record grooves. The mechanism had a wind-up crank, so it was spring-driven. The sound was somewhat scratchy, but it was a good way to hear songs in our early years.

Besides her songs, I remember Mom had many sayings that we now call "Mommy-isms."

*"Sing before seven and cry before eleven."*

*"Red skies in the morning sailors take warning; red skies at night sailors delight."*

*"Säuft bruder säuft, der dollar must noch drauf.";*
*Drink brother drink, the dollar must be spent.*

Ma and Aunt Clara were quite close. They would talk on the phone at least once a week. We would go to see Grandpa Bernard, Grandma Elizabeth, and Clara quite often. After Clara moved to St. Paul, the calls became less frequent because long-distance calls were quite expensive in those days.

In 1951 or 1952, the house of one of our neighbors burned down. I do not remember how much of their personal belongings they were able to save, but the house was completely destroyed. Dad offered them the use of the house on the Altman farm—which was empty at the time—while they got their stuff together and had a new house built. I am not sure how long they were there, but I know it was from early in the year well into spring before they were able to move into their house. I don't know how much rent Dad charged, but they needed a place to live—we had a house available, so we offered it.

# Church

*Immaculate Conception Church, New Munich*

When Great–Grandpa Andreas settled in New Munich, he attended the Immaculate Conception parish. Priests from the St. Johns Abbey of Collegeville—a Benedictine Order founded in 1858—served the parish. Parochial schools were set up sometime later in each community. Neither Freeport nor New Munich had a public school in town when I was going to school. The parochial school was much better than the country school down the road from our house. Religious education was another factor in that decision. When the church decided to establish the parochial schools, quite a few members did not agree with that process. Apparently, Andreas was one of the dissenters.

In 1936, Great-Grandpa and Great-Grandma Hagen (Grandma Job's parents) celebrated their golden wedding anniversary at mass in Freeport and held the family celebration at the farm. It was in Freeport because Sister Annunciata, their daughter, was the organist and music teacher at Freeport. Most people held major celebrations at their homes, and we had the largest house in the extended family.

**Nicholas and Margaret Hagen**

*Get together with the Hagen's in approximately 1950. Living room of our house, after Grandpa and Grandma returned from California. Back row: Jerome Eller, Donna Eller, Mabel Hagen, Eddie, Sally, Minnie, Dolores, Dorothy. Middle row: Sister Annuciata, ---Eller, Margaret Hagen, Lewis Job, Elizabeth Job, Ralph. Front row: Artie (Hidden), Rich, Harold, Clara, Sonny, Ethel.*

We went to Sunday morning mass every week. In the early years—Grandpa's generation, before cars —it was more difficult to get there because they drove the farm wagon or buggy. In the winter with snow on the ground, they drove a sleigh. With snow on the ground, it could be a chore to get to church with horses pulling a sled through fresh snow. Sometimes after a fresh snowfall, the neighbors about two miles to the southeast would put their horses up at our farm, and everyone would ride together as the first set of horses were tired from breaking a track in the fresh snow.

When I was two or three, I went to mass one summer Sunday in New Munich with Ma. I was wearing a sharp white shirt and shorts outfit. Being a two-year-old, I was always fiddling with something. Ma gave me her rosary, and I proceeded to pull it apart by pulling on it over my knees.

Ma was the center of our family's religious life. She usually initiated prayers for meals and other special prayers. During Lent, we took time to say a rosary each day after our evening meal before going out to do the milking. In the earlier years, it was all in German. Later, when there were fewer of us, and we spoke mostly English, we switched to English prayers because we had forgotten the German words. I can remember the year we switched because we kids could not respond to Mom leading the prayers. Dad said it was time to go with the English. Now, I feel bad because I do not even remember the "Our Father" in German.

While Ma was the leader in prayers at home, Dad was always ready for mass on Sundays and Holy Days. He got the car from the garage and was ready to go fifteen minutes before mass to assure we got there in time. There was never a question of if we were going to church; it was strictly a question of when we were going. Both Ma and Dad were committed to going to church every Sunday and Holy Day.

Below is the eulogy that Fr. Hoppe gave at Dad's funeral. Even though it was written for Dad, I think it describes how both Ma and Dad lived their lives:

Ralph L. Job

April 14, 1908–January 21, 1998

**JESUS BEGAN TO TEACH THE CROWDS - (Mathew 5:1)**

As I was at the prayer service last night, here in Sacred Heart Church, in conversation with each of the ten surviving children of Ralph and Wilhelmina Job, each of them knows that we all feel deeply with them at the death of their father. What each of them needs at this time, in addition to the promise of prayer for him and for them, is the assurance that their father, together with Wilhelmina Wensmann Job, have been good examples of Christian living, examples to all of us that religion is not to be lived only on Sunday morning when they are in attendance at Mass, and at their private prayer, but when they have their hands folded in prayer or on their knees.

My knowledge of Ralph Job goes back to May 21, 1929, the day of their marriage in Immaculate Conception Church, New Munich, though I must confess that I did not see him that day. When it came time for marriage, Ralph simply cast his eyes south and a little bit east. Across the Soo Line railroad tracks, to the Ben and Elizabeth Wensmann farm and there found Wilhelmina Wensmann, who lived with him in Christian marriage until January 25, 1987, the day of Minnie's death. My knowledge of him therefore goes back almost seventy years. But in those almost seventy years, I did not have any intimate knowledge of his personal prayer life, though my feeling is that he was always in attendance at Sunday Mass, that he was a prayerful man, and that prayer was a part of his life.

What has impressed me, from speaking to some of the children last night is what I consider a monumental commitment to Christian marriage, from a man who probably was not considered outwardly religious. He received all the sacraments with the exception of Holy Orders, no doubt including Anointing of the Sick in his last days, but it is the Sacrament of

Marriage that he lived daily that I am impressed with. In a small booklet on First Communion published by the Leaflet Missal of St Paul, Minnesota, a single page there outlines all seven sacraments. It has put matrimony in seventh place, but it is a sacrament that seems to have permeated Ralph's entire life, though he may not have seen it that way at all. I want to quote that small paragraph. It says: Matrimony - (the sacrament) by which a man and a woman are able to fulfil the will of God toward each other and bring each to salvation, and in their union bring about an increase of persons who are called to be happy with him (God) forever in Heaven. From whatever time of day Ralph died on Wednesday, I trust that he already knows, in company with the wife who preceded him in death, the great happiness that God has in store for those who "do his will".

The memorial card lists for us Ralph and Minnie's children and their spouses, tells us of the number of their grandchildren and the number of great grandchildren. You have that in your possession already. But, what is most impressive to me is their willingness to be parents of a large family, who in turn have sixty-eight children, and they, in turn, have already have one hundred and ten children. All we had to do was to be aware of those stands in the center aisle of the church as we came up to the front of church last night to see that what was begun with just two people on May 21, 1929, has become a most fruitful tree. They lived their marriage in house and bedroom, (married people need not be a bit ashamed of that), in kitchen and dining room, in the barn and in the field, as well as in the garden and in the workshop. They lived their marriage in act, not just in the words they pronounced that day in New Munich, Mn. Belonging at first to Immaculate Conception Church in New Munich, when World War II came Ralph began to work in Freeport. Since he made that trip each day to town, they transferred their parish allegiance to Sacred Heart Church, Freeport, and he brought along their children so they could attend Sacred Heart School, Freeport, giving their children the opportunity for a parochial school education.

Today's Gospel, that of the eight beatitudes, is introduced by the words of the Gospel which tells us that Jesus began to teach the crowds. That is the lesson that must be for all of us today, as we bring Ralph's body into this church for the Holy Sacrifice of the Mass and then for burial at Sacred Heart Cemetery just as soon as Mass is over. What I was also told last night was that all the grandchildren and the great grandchildren were always welcome in their presence and he took great delight in them. That told me that Ralph, subconsciously, was doing what Jesus did when he allowed and wanted the little children to come to him, and that Ralph was a real teacher in act, not just in word. How powerful when what a person believes is also seen by how a person lives. It's always so easy to talk, but when what one does is in agreement with one's commitment, that speaks loudly and will always command action. You remember the incident in the gospel of Jesus embracing the children and how He blessed them. One source tells us that He played with the children, but he taught the grownups.

I believe that Ralph taught by what he lived, though he may never had said those words: Vatican II. His commitment to marriage and to the Church is an example to his children, to his grandchildren and to his great grandchildren, and to this entire community. I believe that he has entered into his great reward with the Father and the Son and the Holy Spirit, whose names he spoke every day when he made the sign of the cross. May he pray for all of us now as we trust that he in the presence of the Blessed Trinity.

While we were growing up, one tradition at the Freeport parish was to have an outside procession on Corpus Christi, the Thursday after Pentecost. Fr. Linus, all the mass servers, and the choir led the procession—followed by all the parishioners—to three outdoor chapels where the blessed sacrament was displayed for several minutes as a symbol of adoration to God. There were prayers and singing during this procession.

Every year, there was a parish bazaar that we always looked forward to. It usually started right after the last mass, in time for a noon meal, which was usually a gourmet feast. The main feature was the family-style chicken dinner. It was always good, and there was a choice of pies for dessert. We were always stuffed after those meals. There were also kids' games and activities, making it a very eventful day. It was one of many fond memories growing up.

At one of these bazaars, a priest was eating his dinner and observed a young boy who was almost finished but reluctant to get up. After the priest finished his meal, he went to comfort the boy and asked him if anything was wrong. The boy replied that there was nothing wrong, but that there were so many good cookies, and he could not eat anymore. The priest suggested that the boy fill up his pockets, to which the boy replied, "But my pockets are already full."

# Chapter 8

# Kids Growing Up

*The Job children in 1940. Front: Harold, Rich. Middle: Mary Jane, Artie, Eddie, Louis. Back: Sally, Dorothy, Dolores.*

Dolores and Dorothy started school in New Munich. They would walk to the Pfau farm, the neighbors immediately to the west, and ride to school with them in the morning. Dad or Mom would drive into town in the afternoon and bring them home. The next year, Dad started working at the implement dealer in Freeport, and they switched to school there. After switching schools, we altered the system a bit. When Dad was free, he would take us to school in the morning, and Ma would bring us home in the afternoon. When Dad was sawing logs— or during the seasons where there was field work— Ma did both trips.

I can remember being about two years old, in the midsummer approaching evening, when I threw a temper tantrum. I was hauled off to bed to cool off. I believe I cried myself to sleep and slept the night through.

Mom and Dad purchased a piano in about 1942. Dolores came home from school and immediately sat down and began to play it— she must have been taking lessons. I believe all the girls took piano lessons. Louis took violin lessons during grade school. The violin was Dad's, and he encouraged Louis to play it. The older kids heard Dad play and thought he was pretty good. I do not remember seeing Dad play the violin. I remember Louis playing the violin at some school plays, etc. Louis played the cornet in the band in high school. I played the trombone during my high school years.

Once when I was about four or five, I investigated Dad's violin. Before long, I had all the strings of the violin loose and the strings of the bow twisted. When Dad found out, he quickly administered a punishment—that was a musical instrument, not a toy.

Until I was five, the area to the north and east of the house—the orchard—was a weed patch in the summer. The younger kids had our play trails through this patch. The weeds were taller than I was. In about 1950, Dad reseeded grass into the area and mowed regularly during the summer. It looked a lot nicer as a mowed yard, but we missed our play trails.

When Freeport got its siren, we would hear it turned on every day. Harold got pretty good at mimicking it. While milking cows one evening, the siren went off as usual. Then, it went off again. Dad came running out of the shop, wondering what was happening. He laughed pretty hard when he realized it was Harold mimicking it.

We had several dogs growing up, including a dark one named Silver and a collie mix named Dick. They were pretty good dogs. I don't remember what happened to Dick. When I got older, he was gone. We then got a young collie mix. He didn't seem to be very good in that he did not do his job: moving cattle. He would simply stay next to whoever was moving the cattle and not help at all. One Sunday, the boys were hunting—walking through our forty-acre woods—and came out at the Altman farm. As we got into the yard, a small pup came running up to us. The dog could not have been more than two or three months old. He was our first "Sport." He was a good cattle dog and turned out to be a good hunting dog as well. Sadly, he was only three or four years old when he was struck and killed by a milk truck. Dad was very angry, but it happened on the open road, so the driver was not really to blame.

In the 1940s and early 50s, we had several beehives in boxes behind the house. I would sit and watch the worker bees coming and going. I wanted to see how large the pollen sacks on their legs were. I think all of us got stung once or twice when we got caught doing the wrong thing close to the bees. When Eddie was fifteen or sixteen years old, he was stung by a bee on the outside of his left eye. That side of his face swelled up and was very distorted; his eye was almost swollen shut. Dad teased him that he was lucky the bee didn't sting him between the eyes; if it had, he wouldn't have been able to see for a few days.

Invariably, some of the bees would swarm to a new hive. When this happened, we captured the bees and got them into a new hive. In the winter, we stored the hives in an old, detached garage next to the garden. In the summer, the hives would split, and a swarm of bees would migrate to a tree somewhere. The trick was to find the swarm and get the branch cut off without getting stung. Once we got them to an open hive, they usually moved into it without any further coaxing.

On some of the good years, we had four or five hives with three to five supers—smaller boxes on top of the main box—on each hive. Then in the fall, we had to get the bees out of the supers to harvest the honey. We bought a honey extractor that would hold four to six honey frames. We would cut the wax seal at the outer edge, place the frames into the extractor, and turn the crank. The centrifugal force would throw the honey onto the outer shell, where it would run down to the bottom to be put into jars. There were several years when we had very good honey to use on our bread. One winter, none of the hives survived; something wiped out many hives in the area. We never got any bees back after we lost that group.

While we got our honey from our bees, Ma bought syrup in gallon pails. When the pails were empty, they became our lunch pails for school. Lunch usually consisted of some type of sandwich, fruit if available, and a dessert. Hot lunches came to public schools as part of the National School Lunch Act, which passed in 1936. Hot lunches came to our school in about 1948. It was quite an event—the law changed, and the parochial schools were now allowed the same hot lunches that the public schools had had for years. We had a hot noon meal through the rest of our school years. We also got half a pint of milk in a glass bottle. An elderly couple with a good reputation for cooking were the cooks in the early years.

In the earlier years, Mom did a lot of the driving to and from school. Mom and Dad felt that the weather was too unpredictable to let us walk the 3.5 miles every day. The older kids were done with school after the eighth grade. Aunt Clara lectured

Mom and Dad about the need for the kids to get a high school education for the modern world. It evidently worked because Louis started high school in 1951. In the winter of 1950, Dad bought a Chevy three-quarter-ton pickup and started hauling the milk to town in the morning. He dropped us off at school on the way. There were six of us kids crammed into the cab of the pickup with Dad on those rides to town.

Sunday afternoons in the winter were a time to listen to music on the radio. In the earlier years, it was on an RCA radio on the fireplace mantel. Later, they bought a console radio with a phonograph that could play the 33-rpm long-play records, the smaller 45-rpm singles, and the 78-rpm medium-sized records. I enjoyed listening to Gene Autry's radio program on Sunday evenings. He always had some songs and a short western story. Sometime after dinner, a program came on that had the introduction song "Long, Long Ago" sung by a bass soloist. Hearing that song reminds me how much I enjoyed those winter afternoons.

In January of 1948, Dolores flew to Los Angeles to help Louis and his wife Louise. They had just had a baby, which gave them five kids under six years old. It was quite an event in our house because flying was almost unheard of. Dolores returned when Grandpa and Grandma came in June. Dorothy went out there the next year when Grandpa and Grandma left in September. She stayed there until the following spring. Sally went the following year and returned the next spring. That was the winter Grandpa got sick, and Dad flew out there and drove them all back.

In 1950, Dolores started business college in St. Cloud. To earn money, she worked as a waitress at a small luncheon shop just off St. Germain Street and later at the Spaniel Hotel dining room. After graduating from the school, she went to work in Melrose for the Selective Service Office. She was interviewed and offered the job via a reference from someone in the area who knew she was from Freeport and had just finished school. She worked there until she got married in 1953.

In 1951, Dad, Ma, Dolores, and Grandma took a vacation to California in the winter. Grandpa was expecting a postcard, and there was a snowstorm, so he convinced Eddie and Joe Friedel to walk to town after the storm was over, but the roads had not opened yet. Sure enough, there was a card with information on their arrival in California. When they returned, our cousin Jimmy came with them. He spent the next year and a half with us. We had a lot of fun and learned a lot about other different parts of the country from him.

Jimmy brought his hobby of building and flying model airplanes with him. The first airplane he built was a "U-controlled" monoplane. It was approximately eighteen inches. long with a wingspan about the same length. It was controlled by a "U" handle and a pair of wires running to the left wing, which controlled the ailerons for up and down. It was quite exciting to see it going round. He was good at doing acrobatics with it. Unfortunately, he crashed it one afternoon while demonstrating it at the High School in Melrose. He brought home a pile of wreckage.

Art, Louis, Harold, and I all built models of some sort. They were balsa wood frames with special paper glued to them. The special paper covering was coated with a lacquer called "Clear Dope." The construction was quite durable. The best one was a "Fubar," a small model about twenty-four inches long with a thirty-inch wingspan. It was powered by a 0.049cc engine which ran for about thirty seconds and could climb in a circle about 100 feet in diameter. At the end of the powered flight, it would glide in that same circle towards the ground. The objective of the powered start was that it would catch an air thermal during the glide flight, and the circular updraft would carry the plane upwards. This model was quite good at catching the thermals and getting up hundreds of feet. Once on a warm June day, we launched the plane, and it caught a strong thermal wind and climbed so high that we could no longer see it. We were quite disappointed that we had lost our favorite model. A little over a month later, Harold was cutting grain about a half-mile north of the house when he ran into the plane while cutting. Unfortunately, he was not able to stop before he cut the wing in two.

Art built a larger model about thirty-six inches long with a 42-inch wingspan; it was powered by a 0.29cc engine. It was also a very durable plane and, to my knowledge, was still in one piece several years ago. We also spent a lot of time flying this model, and it found thermals well. One overcast winter day, it found a thermal and rose out of sight. We had an address label on it, and a few days later, we got a call from someone several miles away who had found it. They returned it in good condition.

Jimmy stayed until Louis and Louise came for Dolores's wedding in 1953. The most interesting thing we learned from him was building and flying those model airplanes. Also, in 1953, Sally started business college. After she graduated, she took a job with Raymond Trucking.

There were movies every week in Freeport during the summer. The movies showed against the outside of a building with everyone sitting on the ground. During the rest of the year, they were in the town hall on the second floor above the town hall/fire station. It was one of the social activities we looked forward to. We kids could rat around with our friends and have fun.

There were dance halls all over the area. The closest one was the New Munich Coliseum north of New Munich at the intersection of highways US52 and MN237. It was one of the better-attended halls. Others were the Lakeview Ballroom in Avon; the Green Lantern in St. Anthony; the Riverside Coliseum in Richmond; one in Spring Hill; Sauk Center; and St Cloud. In New Munich, there was "old-time dance music" on Tuesday evenings and "modern dance music" on Friday evenings. Mary

Jane says the year she and Buddy got married, there were shower dances, wedding dances, and other celebrations every night of the week at New Munich for several months. There were many nights when the dance halls were packed. On some of the hot summer evenings, it seemed everyone dancing was soaked with sweat.

*The Ralph - Wilhelmina Job Family in 1955. Front row: Dad, Ethel, Richard, Arthur, Clara, Ma. Back row: Louis, Marcella, Mary Jane, Edward, Dolores, Dorothy, Harold.*

# Chapter 9

# Working Around the House and Garden

The original kitchen in our home had a wood stove against an inside wall. The stovepipe ran horizontally across the kitchen to the chimney on the outside of the west wall. The stovepipe would drip on the floor, so one of the early remodeling projects was to move it closer to the chimney to have a shorter stovepipe and fewer problems. We kept the wood for the stove on the back porch on the south side of the house. We had to fill the back porch with small pieces of wood which fit into the cookstove. We piled this wood several rows deep— eight feet long by at least six feet tall—which took up about half the porch. The pile usually lasted most of the winter.

Mom cooked on the woodstove in the small kitchen. She always had pots and pans all over the stovetop. Those stoves had a food "warmer" about two feet above the cooking surface and a water warming reservoir at the right end—which was always kept full to have hot water available. She almost always kept a tea kettle full of water on the stove as well. She got an electric stove in the mid-1950s and used it for most meals. However, in the spring or fall when it was cool in the morning, she would start a fire in the woodstove to "take the chill out" of the kitchen.

The kitchen originally had a pantry with a door. There were shelves on the top and a counter with working space and drawers below. The pantry had the many ingredients necessary to feed a large family. Dad later removed the door and added doors to the shelves, so it looked more like a finished cabinet. Another addition came in the late 1940s when Ma got a refrigerator.

In those years, the water we used came from the cistern in the basement. It was about 16x20 feet in size and about ten feet deep. There were very few years when there was not enough water. The kitchen sink was under a window on the west wall. The hand pump on the sink drew water from the cistern for use. The sink drained directly out through a pipe in the wall, which carried the water away from the house. We got drinking water from the well in the middle of the yard.

Ma did the washing in the basement on a ringer washer. When we were younger, we heated the water from the cistern in a large tub on a kitchen stove down there. When hot, we lifted it in a bucket to the washer and rinse tubs. The wash was then carried out to the clothesline on the east side of the smokehouse. On Mondays, the lines were full of washed clothes. In the winter, the clothes would freeze solid, and we had to bring them indoors to finish the drying process. It was hard work to bring the stiff clothes inside and put them on the clothes rack to dry.

One of the first small appliances Ma got was an electric iron. I remember the old iron pieces, which Ma heated on the surface of the kitchen stove and then used for the ironing job. Mom was a very good seamstress. We believe she had some lessons from a seamstress when she was a girl. Until the 1950s, she made many of the girls' dresses. She had a treadle sewing machine until about 1950 when she got an electric Necchi sewing machine. Dolores kept the pedal-operated machine until she passed away.

Mom's garden was over an acre in size, and she raised countless fruits and vegetables. There were always two or three rows of sweet corn. She planted early lettuce so that we could eat it by mid-May, depending on the weather. Along with the early lettuce, she also had radishes and baby onions. She always had lettuce, onions, radishes, peas, beans, beets, cabbage, pumpkins, rutabagas, and squash. There was always a large strawberry patch as well as a raspberry patch. We always had several rows of peas, beans, and sweet corn which we froze to use later. We picked the sweet corn at just the right stage, and then we cooked, blanched, and cut off the ears, then placed them in freezer bags.

We harvested navy beans in October, which made for good soups and other bean dishes. In the fall, we made the cabbages into sauerkraut. We seasoned the sauerkraut in large twenty-five and thirty-gallon stone crocks. A lot of meals included sauerkraut, and it tasted very good. We had a varied diet, and I don't remember ever going hungry. The garden also had ground cherries that grew wild. They made a delicious sauce for dessert.

The orchard had a Duchess apple tree which was a good eating apple. There were two sour apple trees for canning or freezing; they made good pies and sauces. There was a green apple tree—what I would now call a golden delicious—that kept well and was good for eating in late fall and into the winter. There was also a crab apple tree, several plum trees, and cherry bushes. Some years, we used the hay wagon to load the apples into as we picked them. They were then transferred to the root cellar in the basement; it had a ground floor. They were later made up into sauce or frozen for pies. This is also where we kept the potatoes and carrots. We sometimes covered the carrots with sand or sawdust for longer storage. Ma used to make dried apples, but no one seems to know how she did that.

Mom must have enjoyed gardening because she would spend hours preparing the soil, planting, and hoeing the various plants. One of us would do a rough plowing and once-over with the field cultivator, then Mom took over. On summer days, when the sun was bright, she wore a large-brim straw hat. It had a scarf sewn onto it so she could tie it under her chin and not lose it when it was windy. We always looked forward to the first fruits of each crop. In late spring, we got radishes and baby onions. As the season continued, we enjoyed the young leaf lettuce and early peas. Another highlight was the ear corn. Usually, the field corn was ripe first, and we would have those for a few days. Then, the sweet corn came. In the fall, there were fresh beets, rutabagas, and kohlrabi with our meals. All the girls did their share of the hoeing and weeding and other work necessary for the garden to be fruitful.

Picking chokecherries was a yearly occurrence. We had a grove along the property line with the Shultzenbergs, southwest of the house and across the creek. There were a good number of trees, so we got chokecherry jam and sometimes an abundant harvest of wine. Everyone got involved in picking the berries, and we got to eat quite a few while we picked. After we bought the Altman farm, we found another grove of chokecherry trees on the edge of the field above the spring—it yielded a good number of berries as well. As the girls got older and helped more, they mixed apples and other fruit in with the chokecherries. It made for some very good-tasting jam. My favorites were strawberry-rhubarb and strawberry-apple jam.

Ma and the girls canned a lot of fruits and vegetables from the orchard and garden every year. Before we got the freezer, we kept some meat and other foods in a locker, first in New Munich and later in Freeport. We had to make several stops around town to get food for our meals. Meal preparation was much easier once we got a freezer. Bread, pies, and cakes were in abundance as Ma or one of the girls was always baking something. Normally, there was a sauce or cake for dessert after supper. Birthdays were always special as we usually had ice cream and cake for dessert.

In the fall, we lined the basement shelves with jars of canned goods. After Dad moved out the power plant, he put shelves on the south cistern wall. Those shelves were almost always full by late fall. We ate pretty well off the contents of those shelves and the freezer. The shelves were elm boards and took a definite bow over the years from the weight of the jars. Along with the sauerkraut, Mother also cured pickles in a vinegar solution. There were dill pickles and other thin-sliced pickles, which we put into fruit jars.

Mother used to make several kinds of sausage. There was head cheese, blood sausage, and pork sausage. Out of all the sausages on the market today, there are very few that compare to the pork sausage she made. She would meticulously clean the small intestine from the butchered pigs for the casing. It took hours to get them clean. There was a lot of ground pork and spices in the sausage. Ma smoked the sausages in the smokehouse every year. It was very good. I was never one to eat much of the head cheese or the blood sausage. I just could not quite get past the look of those. When we had the pork sausage, it was usually for Sunday evening supper. We considered it one of the better meals.

In the winter, our Sunday afternoon snack was popcorn popped in the frying pan on the stove. Ma had a large dishpan approximately eighteen inches in diameter and six inches high. It was usually filled heaping full, and we ate it very quickly. On several occasions, Ma would make the Sunday soup in a larger kettle. Then she, Dad, and some of the kids would get into the car and take it to Great–Grandpa and Grandma Hagen for their Sunday lunch. They were living in an "old folks home" by that time. They both lived into their 90s.

# Chapter 10

# The Farm

***Our house from the west***

I was somewhat pleasantly surprised to hear our house referred to as the "Job mansion" in the 1950s while I was in high school. The farmstead was between a road to the north, originally platted as the St. Joe–New Munich road, and a spur of the Soo Line Railroad to the south. The road was not parallel to the railroad tracks as it made a turn to the north at the east edge of our property line; the farmstead has a trapezoidal shape. At its narrowest on the east side, it was approximately 400 feet wide. This was where Mom had her garden —it was over an acre in size. On the west side by the cow yard and a grove of trees, it was approximately 800 feet wide. The railroad track was approximately 200 feet from the back door of the house. The house Grandpa built in 1917 stood at the highest point of the yard and overlooked the rest of the farmstead. The granary, later the shop, and still later the small house, were approximately fifty feet from the railroad track. There was a windmill with a well in the center of the yard. Our farm was unusual in that you could drill down thirty feet with a three-inch hand auger and find water anywhere in the farmstead area. It was simply a matter of getting a well point on the bottom end of the pipe, adding enough lengths of pipe to reach the underground water, and hooking up a pump. We had a well in each of the buildings on the farm except the shop and the machine shed.

*Our house fom the southwest*

Grandpa built the house in 1917. Some facts about the house: He bought the house as a kit from Sears-Roebuck. They dug the hole and foundation too deep, so the house had a very high ceiling basement. They had a lot of rain when they dug the foundation, and the foundation trench was full of water. They dug a trench to drain most of the water and started filling it from the high side, causing the water to spill out at the low end. They started running low on cement for the foundation, so they thinned the mixture. That is supposedly why the basement walls were always gritty. They made the foundation higher than it was supposed to be, which made the house sit very high in the yard.

The house had a bathroom in it, but there were no fixtures until the late 1940s. There was a white cabinet in it that held linens. The house did not have running water until Dad put in an electric pressure pump and a connection to the kitchen sink in the early 1940s. The well was already dug but was not used until the electric pump was installed. The kitchen sink drained straight out the side of the house onto a grassy area. We took baths on Saturday evening in a large, galvanized tub which we brought into the kitchen and filled with water. The baths started with the small kids first and then one by one until everyone was clean. In the first year or so—when we put the bathtub and sink in that room—we heated the hot water for the baths on the kitchen stove and carried it to the bathroom.

In the late 1940s, we added a bathtub, a sink, and a toilet stool to the bathroom. It was a rather large undertaking as we had to install the septic tank on the east side of the house and the drain line dug to the road ditch to the north. The kitchen sink was also drained into this system, but it ended up below the level of the septic tank and drained straight outside. In about 1947, Dad added an electric water heater to the system. I remember it was rather large as Dad would not have gas in the house. It was on a timer so that it would not run while chores, milking, and other such work, was being done as it took a lot of power to operate.

The outhouse was in several locations while we were growing up. It was never too far from the house because it could be a miserable trek in extremely cold weather. The last location was at the southeast corner of the granary.

*The barn from the west. No one knows who this woman is or what she was doing.*

Dad began to do all the farming in 1928 when Grandpa went to California to arrange to live with his brother George. He and Ma then began farming it together in 1929 when they got married. At that time, the smokehouse was east of the house, and the sawmill was further east in what is now the northwest corner of the garden, just south of the road. There was a single-car garage on the west edge of the garden, almost in the center. There was a windmill in the center of the yard—some concrete foundation remnants were still there in the early 1940s—and the barn and the hog barn were to the west. The granary was on the south side of the railroad tracks; it also included a stall for the horses. Where the machine shed now stands, on the west end, there used to be a plain shed. Where the sawmill was, there was a building that held an icehouse and a workshop. The chicken coop was to the west of that building. There was also a straw pile where the manure pit is now. There was a small shed under the straw pile. In the early 1940s, we kept some hogs there. Loose straw was no longer available after Dad started combining small grains in 1940; that shed then lost its straw cover and was finally torn down.

Grandpa and Grandma wanted to spend more time in California and make some investments, so they asked Dad to purchase the farm from them in 1938. He had the loan arrangements made through the bank in Freeport, but when he went back to close the deal, they told him that someone else had insisted they came first—"Erst come Ich." He then went to the bank in Melrose to get the loan. The original purchase did not include the forty acres of woods about half a mile northeast of the farm buildings and pasture of the Altman farm.

Grandpa had purchased a "home electric plant"— an engine-powered generator—in the early 1920s.

The home plant also had a "line shaft" to which the milk machine and cream separator—a McCormick-Deering unit—we could clutch on as needed. The plant had a series of batteries; in those days, the batteries were in glass cases. The house could then have electric power from the batteries late into the evening. We used the cream separator in the milk house of the new barn starting in late 1949. After 1950 or 1951, we no longer separated cream from the milk in the summer.

*The northeast corner of the barn with the
milkhouse*

The original barn did not have a drive-through for hauling manure, so Dad added a door on the north end that made loading and hauling manure a little easier. Adding the door was difficult as the concrete foundation was eighteen inches thick. The barn also had a water tank on the hay floor, and we pumped it full every afternoon so the cows could drink from water cups—double bowl units—one between two stalls. We kept one team of horses at the south end of the barn.

On April 30, 1938, the barn burned down—it was the day after Dolores's birthday. Shortly after a train had gone through, Sally was the first to see the smoke and fire. At that time, coal-fired steam engines drove the trains. A stray spark from the coal fire was not unusual. Dad and Tony Tillman were working in the field, and one of the older kids ran out to tell them. Dad and Tony were able to salvage the home plant, the batteries, the milk machines, and the separator. Considering that the home plant was an engine and generator unit, it was a big job to get the home plant out of the barn. Tony spilled some acid from the batteries on his pants. He had to go home and get a different pair because the acid had eaten through the ones he had on.

The morning after the fire, Dad hosed the ashes from the concrete floor of what had been the barn, and they milked the cows in the open air. They milked the cows that way until Dad sold off some cows to get enough money to build a new barn south of the house. He was a smart enough businessman to sell the cows with the contingency that he got some of the calves from the first year. Those calves and other sources were to rebuild the herd he needed to build a sustainable farming operation.

After the fire, Dad installed the home plant in the basement of the house, and it ran there until REA (Rural Electrification Administration) came through later that year. The home plant was in a narrow area between the cistern and the south wall of the basement under the kitchen. Dad moved it out of this basement location in the early 1940s. It must have been quite a job to get the plant into and then out of the basement, as it was about twelve steps down. I never learned what became of the power plant. REA came through with electric power in late 1938. Dad hooked up to the electricity as soon as it was available. It was a welcome change from the very noisy home plant—the kitchen floor vibrated when the home plant engine ran.

They built a new barn that could house fifteen cows, which later became the granary at the south side of the farmstead just north of the railroad tracks. This barn had a tin roof; I imagine that was to protect from sparks from the railroad steam engines. There was a lean-to on both the north and south sides for young cattle and other animals. The well in this location had problems periodically; while there was plenty of water available, the well point became plugged with fine sand, resulting in reduced water flow. The pipe for this well then had to be pulled up and the point flushed of sand or replaced. During this time, we kept the horses in a barn adjacent to the granary across the railroad tracks.

In 1940, Dad moved the sawmill from northeast of the house to the northwest, west of the driveway, and south of the road. He moved it because the sawmill's previous location was always muddy after it rained. He dismantled an old shed to make room for the sawmill. He added a large machine shed foundation and walls. Some of the studs and siding for the new shed came from the old shed. For the first year or so, only the walls stood. During the war years (1941–1945), a farmer could only spend $1000. That may explain why it took several years to build the machine shed.

Young cattle were in a pen at the west end of this building. During the coldest part of the winter, there was a makeshift roof of tamarack poles covered with straw for the cattle. We added the roof in late 1945 or 1946. Herb Hennen, the lead carpenter and later owned of the lumber yard in Freeport, had seen curved truss rafters built, so he used that construction for the shed. The rafters were a fabricated two-ply made from 1x6 eight-feet-long elm boards cut at a radius for the roof curve and nailed together to make the truss frame. The roof boards were 1x8. The roofing material was a tar paper material with green-colored, fine stone pebbles embedded in the asphalt. We added the doors to the west of the sawmill in later years.

Dad and Mom wanted a garage close to or in the house, so in the early 1940s, he propped up the front porch and dug out the area under it for a garage. He dug with an invention the Pfau brothers, our neighbors on the farm to the west, called a front-end loader, which used hydraulics to operate the loader lift arms. Mom got her garage as part of the house, and the front porch was a little sturdier after that. There was a drawback to that garage—we had to walk outside the house to get to it. There was not an opening into the house as the basement floor was about six feet below the level of the garage. The ceiling of the garage, which was also the floor of the front porch, was concrete, and because the garage was not heated—and the west half was exposed—the floor was always very cold in the winter. Before Ma got the freezer, the garage was her refrigerator in the spring and fall and a temporary freezer in the winter.

*The machine shed. Sawmill is in the open area to the left.*

*The original front entrance. Left to right: Conrad, Lewis, Elizabeth, Sophie, and ?*

In 1943, he built a larger barn—approximately 26x44 feet—to the southwest of the machine shed where he could accommodate twenty milk cows. The foundation was dug by hand. The night before they were to pour the concrete for the foundation, it rained. They put a drain in the lowest end and started filling the highest end. Eventually, the concrete pushed the water out of the foundation trench.

*New barn in 1943*

The barn was a clay tile structure with curved laminated rafters. The shingles were a hard-slate asbestos—a material that did not burn easily. It was one of the few structures in the area with that type of shingle. There was a well in the southeast corner, as well as room for the cream separator. The water system for the cows used a closed tank in the haymow with straw bales piled around it to keep it from freezing in the winter. The cows had individual water cups, and the pump was a pump-jack style. I think the pump ran automatically; in which case, there would have been a float and switch in the tank to turn it on and off. It seems that the hay barn part of it was always too small. It did not have the typical haymow door—we had to send all the hay and straw in via a bale elevator through a man-sized door—3x8 feet—on each end.

In 1944, Dad found a wood stave silo that one of the neighbors was replacing. He, and likely a crew, dismantled the silo and set it up at the southeast corner of this barn. It was filled with corn silage, was a welcome addition to the cows' diet, and improved their milk production. In the summer of 1945, the silo was blown down in a storm. He re-erected it and filled it with silage that fall. In the summer of 1946, another storm blew it down again. Since he didn't feel like re-erecting it every year and already knew where he was going to build his large barn, he had a clay tile 14x30 foot silo built. He had enough silage for his cows that winter.

The silo was filled with corn shocks which were hauled to the silage cutter at the base of the silo. A six-inch pipe carried the silage into the silo. In those years, the corn stalks for silage were cut in the field with a corn binder—which, like the binder for the grain, cut the corn stalk just above the ground, tied eight to twelve stalks into a bundle, and then dropped it on the ground. Unlike the grain bundle, this bundle was heavy. It took a good amount of effort to pick up the shock with a pitchfork and load it onto a wagon. It was then hauled to the cutter at the silo and fed into the cutter. The twine which tied these shocks had to be cut and removed, as it was not good for the cows.

In 1948, Uncle Al got a field chopper which chopped the corn into silage in the field. The unloading then consisted of forking the silage into the hopper of the blower which literally blew the silage into the silo. It was a lot less work than handling the corn shocks multiple times.

During those years, we almost always had a pile of hay and straw bales next to the old granary to the south of the railroad tracks. We had a canvas tarp with which we covered the top to reduce spoilage. Many years, the canvas was not long enough, and we improvised by piling loose meadow hay on top and weighing it down with baling wire with short slabs of wood on the end to keep it in place. In the 1950s, after the granary building had collapsed completely, we cleaned up that area and turned it into a field.

From 1942 to 1950, we kept the horses and young cattle in a pole barn Dad built on the original barn foundation. The horses were just inside the door on the south end, as they had been in the original barn. There were two separate pen areas, one for the yearlings and one for the two-year-old heifers. A tank—filled twice per day from the well and pump in the chicken coop—watered the animals in that barn. We switched the pump on by a manual switch, and someone had to watch until the tank was full and then shut it off. We sold that barn and it was moved to the Friedel farm in the mid-1950s.

The barn also had a set of doors on the north end, so when we cleaned out the manure, we would drive the manure spreader through the barn to load the manure into it by hand. The manure was usually six inches to a foot deep by the time we cleaned it out, so it was an all-day job to get it all loaded and spread in the field. Once we boys were over eight years old, we were part of the loading crew for these jobs. In the years before 1950, we used the horses to haul the manure into the field and spread it. Once there was snow on the ground, we used a sled to haul the manure into the field. At least two people went along to spread it by hand in the field. The horses pulled the sled slowly while the guys spread it around.

We built the shop in 1947 with a large one-piece door to accommodate Dad's airplane. It was a 40x40 foot clay tile structure with curved truss rafters and roof. We used the same style rafters and tar paper roofing material as on the machine shed. Finishing the concrete floor in it was quite a challenge. Dad and at least one mason were working at it until very late in the evening on the day they poured it. The large one-piece door was 8x36 feet. It had five tracks in the ceiling to allow us to raise the door to the roof and push the airplane in. Years later, we split the door in two with one ten-foot and one 25-foot door. In late 1948, there were a few sows with a litter kept in the shop for a few months.

In 1949, we built the big barn—it was 36x110 feet. Dad had spent years figuring out how he wanted the barn layout and cattle moving pattern, and he had built a scale model of the barn before he built the real thing. Dad and Lawrence Sherping—a farmer about a mile north of us who wanted a new barn and so collaborated with Dad—built the same size barns with the same general construction. However, Lawrence opted for more milk cow stalls than the thirty-two Dad had planned. The structure was again the clay tile but with a reinforced tile/concrete hay floor. Since all hay and straw was now baled, the haymow was only twenty-two feet high compared to the older style hip-roofed barns where the haymow was thirty-five or forty feet high. It was fun watching them build the barn. There was always a crew of people around. It took approximately two weeks for a crew of three or four bricklayers to lay the tile for the walls of the structure.

*The big barn, built in 1949. The silo was built before the barn in 1947. The chicken coop is at the left edge of the picture. Note the log piles coming well past the center of the yard.*

The rafters for this barn could not be the same truss type used on the machine shed and the shop, as there was a need for a lot of hay bale storage. So, they devised three-ply, 1x8 inch, six-foot-long oak and ash boards that they cut on a 22-foot radius on the radial arm saw that Herb Hennen had at the lumberyard. They cut the logs in the forty acres of woods Dad owned. They sawed the boards for the rafters and piled them in the shop to dry—they kept the shop heated for this purpose. Later, they constructed the rafters in the shop. After they cut each board on the radius, they placed the pattern on the saw bed so they could trim the boards to fit and then nail them together. They then put the boards into large piles for the construction process, which was quite simple. They marked a 22-foot radius on the floor and laid out the boards: first one ply of oak, then the center ply of ash—they nailed these two piles together with short nails. Then, they added the third ply of oak and nailed the rafter from that side. They then turned over the rafter and nailed it from the other side. They piled up the finished rafters until they reached a convenient working height. Then, they nailed shortboards vertically to the piles to keep the stack in place until they finished the rafters.

When Lawrence Sherping had finished the foundation for the barn, he decided to move his corn crib further from the new barn. When they lifted a corner to block up his corn crib, dozens of rats scuttled out from under it. If they continued, the rats would just find another building on the farmstead to dig under. He had a roll of wood lath snow fence with which they ringed the corn crib. They doubled the fence back on itself, so there was no place large enough for a rat to scurry through.

Two guys with shotguns surrounded the crib up and lifted it. When the rats came running out from underneath, they got shot. It took over a half-hour to kill all the rats. The guys that did the shooting said that their gun barrels were hot from firing them so much.

In the spring, when the frost was going out of the ground, most of the roads turned into a quagmire. Dad demonstrated this on one occasion when he took his hands off the steering wheel and, for almost a mile, let the car run in the ruts in the road. Another time, there was a major frost boil in the middle of the road where it ran through the low-swampy area approximately one mile south of town. This one took up almost half of the road. It presented a challenge to get past it without sliding into the ditch. One year, one of those became a hole in the road for a day.

Spring thaw was always a waiting time as the melting snow would fill up the low swamp area across the road north of the house. On years with a lot of snow, that area became a lake, so there were only a few hundred feet of bare ground north of the road. The fence which ran through the middle of it was usually underwater during this time. It then became a waiting game as to when the ice in the culverts under the railroad would thaw, and water would start flowing through the creek. The creek flowed into Getchel's Creek, which is a part of the Sauk River basin. If the weather was cold, it could take more than a week. When we were younger, that seemed like a very long time. It usually took more than a few days for the water to flow down the creek. I also learned later that the swamp/meadowland north and west of this lowland also drained via this lowland. So, since this lowland had an open waterway to the one across the road from our house, it was likely that the water had to accumulate before the ice in the culverts under the railroad track melted.

*Granary (Original replacement barn 1938–1939)*

*The barns—chicken coop, new barn, and hog barn*

# Chapter 11

# Working on the Farm

*Loading hay by hand (1870?)*

The farm was a typical farm of the 1900s. It had workhorses—in the early years, there were at least two teams of two. There were milk cows, pigs, and chickens. Typical crops were wheat, oats, corn, and potatoes. There were apple trees, plum trees, and cherry bushes for fruit.

Dad was a very hard worker. He would lead us in whatever work we had to do that day and assign tasks for each of us. When we boys were old enough to do light work, Dad assigned us chores to do. He taught us to do certain jobs, and we did them well. He also expected us to be in the barn during morning and evening chores once we were old enough—between six and eight years old. We helped with the milking and feeding of the animals. He was very good at showing us better and easier ways to accomplish tasks.

When I was about five or six years old, I remember several times riding on the hay wagon, loaded with bales, coming home for dinner. One time, there were six or seven of us riding on the hay wagon with the bales. Horses drew the hay wagon in those years. When we reached the yard, we stopped, and everyone except one person, the hired man who put up the horses over the noon hour, ran for the house for our dinner.

Dolores remembers crawling up into the silo and pitching out enough silage to feed the cattle when she was six to eight years old. Another job we had when filling the silos was to be in the silo and guide the blower pipe outlet to fill the silo evenly. At that time, a corn binder cut the corn and tied eight to twelve stalks into a bundle (shocks). We then loaded the shocks onto a hay wagon and fed into the silage chopper at the silo. These shocks were forty to sixty pounds each, and it was a lot of work to get the silage in the silo.

We all wore yellow work gloves as the weather got cooler. For cold weather, we always had a pair of woolen mittens that went inside a pair of leather or felt outer mittens so the wool would last longer. They did a good job of keeping our hands somewhat warm. There were some very cold days when we still could not keep our hands warm. The boys all wore bib overalls when outside. During the cold weather, we wore a larger pair over the first pair. A jacket was the normal outerwear, but when it turned cold, we wore a heavy coat on top. We always had winter caps with earflaps for the cold weather. The caps we wore were always fitted for our size. Fortunately, there were no "one size fits all" caps then. I can remember walking from the house to the barn and the snow crunching under my boots as I walked. As we got older, coveralls became available, and they became the outerwear item for cold weather.

Ma served us lunch every working day. When lunch arrived, we stopped working and dug in. We wiped our hands clean on gloves or a rag if available. This lunch usually consisted of a sandwich, something to drink, and some dessert. Sometimes, we would hold a small piece of sandwich or cookie between our thumb and forefinger for Sport to pick it with his eye teeth; we enjoyed sharing our food with him. I can remember that when we were doing chores when milking was going on, we boys would drink milk out of a milk can cover.

*Southwest corner of the barn*

Since our farm was primarily a dairy farm, the cows got the most attention. The cows were always fed and milked at 6:oo AM and 6:oo PM. We cleaned the dairy barn every day, so the manure would not interfere with the cows' ability to lay down to rest. There were several times when we had to dump the manure outside the barn because we could not get into the fields to spread it due to snow. Although we did not have actual records of the individual production from each cow, we knew which ones were the best producers. We had one cow that was appropriately named "Outlaw," as we would have to retrain her to stand still for the milk machine every year after calving. As she freshened, she would start by kicking off the milk machine for several weeks. We put up with her because she was one of our best milk producers; I believe she was in service for over ten years.

In the fall, after we cut the corn for silage or picked the ears, we pastured the cows in the cornfields. That was also the time of the year when our cows were calving. Many times, we found that one of the cows had calved during the day and was not with the herd. When that happened, we would go out in the car—or in later years, the pickup—as it had better lights than the tractor with which to find the animals. Invariably, they were in one of the remote areas of the field furthest distance from the farmyard. Several times, I recall that one was found next to the wildlife area we called the Tamarack.

One year, one of our neighbors lost his dairy herd to a disease. Dad sold him several of our cows to help him rebuild his herd. I remember Dad telling him that he was getting some of our average cows, not our best.

Being a dairy farm, we always had bulls. Holstein bulls have a reputation for getting mean and destructive as they get older. One year, we had a bull that wreaked havoc on the barnyard fence and then would go for a walk where he wanted. One time, this bull headed east along the road towards the Friedel place. Dad was very mad and got into the car with Eddie —this was before we had the pickup—and headed the bull off before the bull got to the Friedel's yard. When they finally got it turned around, the bull ran down the middle of the road. Dad rammed the bull several times with the car bumper to communicate that it needed to go home. It seems that ended his wandering ways for that winter. I believe that we sent him off to the stockyard for slaughter the next year.

Dad told other stories of bulls destroying their 2x8 and 2x10 plank pens in the barns. When Dad designed the bullpen in the new barn, he used 1.25 and 1.5-inch galvanized piping for the pen wall. One bull liked to make his entrance to his pen from the middle of the yard. He would charge through the open door into the barn and slide in the manure on the floor. One time, we had cleaned out and placed fresh straw on the floor, and the bull did its usual charge into the barn. This time, however, when it hit the straw on the floor, it did not stop easily because the straw was slippery. The bull slid all the way to the pen wall and hit the piping. The bull was a very good size, and it had so much momentum that it bent a couple of the pipes. It did not charge into the barn after that.

One neighbor had a brown, Swiss bull that was very gentle. It had a ring in its nose, and our neighbor would often hook a lead rope to the ring and lead it where he wanted it to go. One time, as he was leading the bull to another neighbor, it turned on him. Fortunately, he had dehorned the bull, but the farmer suffered several broken ribs and various bruises and scratches. He did not trust any bull after that incident.

We had a one-row, two-horse, team-drawn cultivator and a two-row, three-horse, team-drawn unit. Both required the driver seated in the rear on a stamped metal pan seat to steer the cultivator shovels, centering them on the rows. From the time I was old enough to remember, we had only one team of horses, so we only used the one-row unit. I know Ed did a lot of cultivating with it, but Dorothy and Art both remember doing that as well. I also heard that the job was very boring, and the operator was prone to falling asleep. There were basket muzzles to keep the horses from eating the corn stalks; they would grab a stalk and pull the entire stalk up for food. The baskets would also keep flies out of the horses' noses.

Speaking of horses, we had horses and used them on the farm every day into the 1950s. In the years before 1940, there were two teams available. After 1940, we used and kept only one team. After several years of little use, the last two were finally butchered for mink meat in 1956 or 1957. They were the primary power for planting and cultivating corn. They also did all the pulling for the hay wagons from the field to the barns or stacks. One time, Harold took a team of horses home when something spooked them, and they started running. Harold took his job very seriously, so he did not let go of the reins and ended up getting dragged along the ground. When asked why he didn't let go of the reins, he simply said, "I was supposed to take them home."

In late February or March of every year, we got chicks for the next year's chickens, roosters to butcher when fully grown, and hens for laying. One year, we put the chicks in the upstairs of the house for several weeks. After that, the old single-car garage next to the garden became the brooder house. The brooder was a large, insulated sheet with a heating element or lamp in it and a soft canvas covering the sides. The canvas was slit every few inches so the small chicks could get in and go out as they wanted. Their food was in small trays, and there were waterers around the sides. We got 500 to 600 unsorted chicks every year.

As the chickens grew, they could roam outside but we put them into the house every night to avoid wild animals. When the roosters grew big enough, Ma would butcher them in bunches. It was a lot of work for her and the girls, but we always had fresh chicken meat. A lot of it went to fried chicken. I remember it was very good. Of course, when there were all or most of us at home, it took several chickens to feed our hungry family.

For ten years or more, we had a pair of sheep. They could roam in the pasture and sometimes the yard. Their wool was the source for a lot of mittens, socks, sweaters, and quilts for our beds. We sheared them once per year. We cleaned and washed the wool then put it aside for whatever it was to be made into. Usually, that involved carding the wool to separate the fibers. Mom also had a spinning wheel, and she spun a lot of the wool into yarn. That went first to make heavy socks and mittens for the winters. Next came sweaters, and then, as time allowed, Ma made quilts from what remained.

For several years in the 1950s, we hauled small pigs to the Altman farm and let them run in a fenced pasture there and feed. Getting them there when they weighed a few pounds was easy, but catching them and loading them into the back of the pickup at the end of the summer when they weighed close to 100 pounds gave us a good workout.

Dad bought a grey Twin City model KT tractor in 1936. We unloaded it from a truck at the bank behind the house. Tractors in those years were already equipped with rubber tires, but the wagon wheels were converted to car size tires in approximately 1947. Minneapolis Moline made the models R and Z in the late 1930s. There were some model U tractors produced before World War II production switched to producing machines for the war. These models continued after the war for several years.

*Twin City KT tractor and MM Model 69 combine in approximately 1940.*

Danger was a subject that Dad taught us about early and often. Most farm machines are dangerous. You had to be aware of what the dangers were and how to avoid them. We had very few serious injuries while working. One thing that got particular emphasis was driving a tractor through a road ditch. He warned us to reduce the power as we climbed up the incline coming out of the ditch. That was where many people got hurt or killed as the tractor would tip over backward if they tried to accelerate on the climb out of the ditch. In reviewing farm accidents during the latter part of my career, rear upsets resulting in a fatality were still occurring.

Before Dad bought the combine in 1940, a threshing machine and a good-sized crew did the threshing. The grain was first cut with a binder which cut the stalks, gathered them into a bundle, and tied the bundle—approximately six inches in diameter—and dropped the bundle onto the ground. Then, the farmer would gather five to seven bundles and form a shock where the grain could dry and be somewhat protected from rain. Our crew was usually a minimum of six people—one to three crews of two men each—and almost always a group of neighbors. They would load the bundles onto wagons drawn by horses and bring the loaded wagons to the threshing machine.

The threshing machine was usually parked somewhere in a farmyard where the farmer would have convenient access to the straw when he needed bedding for the livestock. A steam engine drove the threshing machine in the early days. In the later years, a farm tractor pulled it with a long, six-inch-wide, flat, belt pulley. We unloaded the grain shocks from the wagons into a conveyor which fed the bundles into the threshing machine. The threshing machine had a cylinder with special bars that beat the grain from the stalks and separated the grain from the straw. The modern combines today still use the same concept of the "rasp" bar to remove the grain from the stalk or the corn from the ear. We blew the straw and chaff over a small shed where we usually kept the hogs. That barn was usually very warm in the winter as the inside was well insulated by the straw and heated by the animal body heat. We loaded the grain into a grain box on another wagon and then unloaded into granaries to use as feed for the livestock.

While the men were doing the threshing work, the ladies of the farms involved got together at the farm and made the noon meal, afternoon lunch, and evening meal for the crews. It was a very labor-intensive but social gathering. If the weather was good, the threshing job would get done in one to two days. Grandpa and Grandma Wensmann lived about a mile away, and they were always part of the neighborhood threshing crew.

We always had a few acres of wheat along with the oats and barley; we put the wheat in a small pen in the granary during the harvest. It was later taken to the mill in Freeport for them to make into flour. The flour came home in fifty to seventy-pound sacks with the Freeport Roller Mill's Swaney White Flour label on them. Ma used the sacks to make clothes for the kids.

Dad bought the first combine in 1940. He converted the binder into a windrower to cut the grain and windrow it by removing the bundler and knotter mechanism and simply delivering a swath at the end of the machine. That was the year that

Dad convinced all the neighbors that combining was the way to thresh grain. It rained a little almost every evening through the harvest season. Dad would wait until late afternoon and then start combining his grain; he could combine for a few hours until late afternoon-evening. While it still took him a relatively long time to put up his grain, he was done long before any of the neighbors because they had to wait for the weather to change to be dry for a week or more so the bundles of shocked grain would dry.

We had a baler for as long as I can remember—the first one, purchased in 1939, was a McCormick-Deering. It required a person to feed the hay into the plunger area with a fork. The divider between the bales was a block of wood with a place for the wires. If the woodblock did not go fully into the bale chamber, the knife on the plunger would chop the block in two. Obviously, you had to have a few extra blocks available. In 1942, Dad bought a Case wire tie baler. It required a minimum crew of three to run it; a tractor driver, the main fork handler—the forks were a grooved rectangular metal frame to hold the wires—and the wire tie person. Dorothy still remembers sitting in the wire tie position and having the dust from every stroke of the plunger wash over her. The person handling the main fork position did a lot of work. They had to load the forks in the trip mechanism and trip the completion of a bale, which sent the fork in between slabs in the bale chamber. Then, after the wire tie person tied off the bale, he had to pull the fork out from between the bales just before the end of the bale chamber. I can remember more than once when we had to stop the operation because the fork was jammed between the bales. Then, two people would manually—with brute force—pull the fork out of the chamber. Imagine doing the main fork job for 500 bales a day; it was a lot of work. The wires were routed so that the loop end went in on one side of the fork, attached to the fork as someone pushed it between the bales and fed the straight end in on the other side. This baler was one of the last ones available because the country switched all manufacturing over to war production items.

Dorothy tells of times when baling hay in a meadow, the tires of the baler would be wet as they moved along. I can remember getting stuck several times when the ground was too soft. We hooked a team of horses to the front of the tractor pulling the baler and then went through the soft spot. We did this later with a second tractor in front of the tractor-baler pair to get through these spots. Sometimes, we unhooked the trailer with bales from behind the unit to get through.

We used that baler until 1953 when we bought an MM wire tie baler. Dad used it until he found that some of the short pieces of wire, cut off at each knot, ended up in the cows' stomachs. The vet proved it to him with a magnetic sound instrument; almost every cow had wire in its stomach. We got a twine baler that year—1957 or 1958. When we baled for our own use, we always stacked it on the hay wagon. If we dropped the bales in the field, there was too much chance the bales would get wet before you got them all picked up. Dad proved it was easier to dry the hay in a windrow than to get a hay bale dry.

As long as we had the hand wire tie baler, we collected the wires from the bales once we had opened them and took them to a straightener Dad had made. It was basically a vise for the straight end with a hook on a lever for the loop end of the wire. We locked the straight end in the vice, hooked the loop on the hook, grabbed the lever at the top end, and pulled until the wire was straight. We reused a lot of baling wire over the thirteen or so years we did hand tie. This straightener mechanism was in the basement until we built the shop, then we moved it and the other tools to the shop.

Since we had one of the few balers in the area through the war years and a few years after, Dad started custom bailing for neighbors. It was not unusual during the summer to have a bailing crew gone from home on the good weather days during the haying season. In 1947-1948, we did custom bailing until the manufacturers finally got enough equipment to the farmers.

After the road was rebuilt in approximately 1950, we always cut and baled the hay in the road ditches. Sometimes, we also cut meadow hay from the Pfau's lowland when they had excess hay. Some of the banks on the side of the road were approximately a 45-degree slope; it was a chore to cut the hay with a tractor. For several years after, we bought the Altman farm and cut the meadow hay in the lowland that Altman owned about a mile south, adjacent to Getchel's creek. For some reason, Dad never bought that land.

Farmers almost all had bucksaws to cut firewood from small trees or treetops. These small logs burned a long time, so we preferred them for very cold winter nights. A new circular bucksaw blade was about thirty inches in diameter. It was a mean machine as it had no guard over the blade—quite a few people lost fingers, part of a hand, or an arm to them. We had one of these as well. It took at least two people to run the cutting operation and several more people to bring the slabs or tree limbs to the people doing the sawing. Dad used slabs from the sawmill for most of the firewood. It was a big chore to cut the slabs into firewood lengths because once the slabs close to the bucksaw were cut up, we either had to move the bucksaw or carry the slabs to the saw.

In the 1940s, Dad built the bucksaw onto the front of his tractor. The saw was at the left front corner, and the belt drive from the tractor pulley was on the right. The saw used the same drive shaft and bearings as the bucksaw but was bolted to mounting brackets at the front of the tractor with rails running back to the rear axle on each side for stability. The person operating the saw stood to the outside of the table beam, and one or more persons held the slabs or cordwood limbs. When the cut was complete, the operator pitched the chunk of wood onto a pile—or most of the time onto a wagon—to bring it to a woodpile close to the house. The operator and the first holder person usually were only a few feet from the saw, and by the end of a day, their ears were ringing. Because this involved a lot of pushing and pitching, one was in pretty good physical condition doing these jobs. If you were not, you were sore for a few days. Neither the saw nor the belt had shields to keep someone out of them; Dad taught us at an early age that they were very dangerous. When Dad bought the new MM "model U," he rebuilt the frame to fit on that tractor. That bucksaw got a lot of use. In the 1940s, he built an electric motor-driven cut-off saw at the end of the lumber roll. We cut the slabs into firewood size and loaded them onto hay racks so we could move and unload them on the woodpile.

Every fall, we cleaned up all the trees that we had cut for lumber or that had blown down. We usually wanted about 15–20% of our firewood in logs for the late-night fires. We could cut at least two wagon loads of wood in an afternoon—this was usually done on Saturdays when we were out of school. The wagons were 8x16 feet hay racks with sixteen-inch-high sideboards, so we could pile a large amount of wood on a load. Using the treetops and other small limbs in this manner, we kept the woods clear of debris.

With a crew usually made up of kids, Dad would cut the slabs from the sawmill into firewood pieces twelve to eighteen inches long on a bucksaw. He then would run the wagon load to town to deliver to people still heating with wood or people using wood to "take the chill out of the house in the morning." Sometimes, the kids going to school would ride home in the wagon. I remember once riding home from school in a wagon with the grain box full of seed grain. Elmo Laing's older kids rode along; they were living in the second small house on the Pfau farm at the time. Dorothy remembers the adults talking about using the sorghum press and boiler to make sorghum molasses. It was a very tedious and demanding process. The pan for evaporating the moisture is still in the machine shed, tied to the rafters. Several of us remember the rolls for the press being in the junkyard; we sold them as scrap along the line.

As most farms do, we had a junk pile; it was behind the granary. Over the years, it accumulated a lot of scrap iron. There were several old farm tools like a hay saw and a loose hay fork to lift a small pile of hay into a barn. Later, the forks gave way to slings of two strands of rope that could pull a larger pile of loose hay into the haymow.

Dad bought a welder in about 1950 and used it for repairs. I believe all of us boys learned to weld and used it on occasion. Grandpa had trouble with the light flash and smoke from the welder, so he would hunker behind his car or go for a walk when welding was being done.

After Dad bought the Minneapolis–Moline G4 combine in 1950, he wanted a swather with a wider cut than the six-foot converted binder. In the winter of 1951 to 1952, he built a twelve-foot pull-type swather. The main beam was a four-inch steel tube, and it carried the far end very well. It made the combining task a little easier in that we did not have to drive it around the field as often.

One time while installing the cutter bar on the forage harvester, I asked Dad how tight the bolts had to be. His reply was "Fest und dan noch mahl rum"—tight and then one more turn. Art asked the same question and got the same answer. On a later occasion, he turned a bolt so tightly that it broke.

*Dad swathing grain with the 12-foot swather he built in approximately 1957.*

*Eddie swathing grain on his farm. Note that the trees in the background to the left are the forty-acre woods Andreas bought.*

In the mid-1950s, Owatonna Manufacturing came out with a self-propelled swather/windrower. This gave Dad the itch to have one, but he thought the purchased units were too expensive. He decided to build his own. He also thought the small drive wheels on the purchased units—about 7.50x16 tires—were too small, so he decided to build his unit with small manure spreader drive wheels. They were about 8x24 tires which drove much better in soft fields. I can remember when he brought the drive transmission from Owatonna Manufacturing home to install on the unit. It took me a long time to understand how these units with the clutch on each end to drive or release each wheel worked. The drive from the engine was a variable speed V-belt unit, which worked quite well. It also took me until after I took my engineering design courses in college to understand how the spring-loaded driven pulley set would match the drive input from the engine output shaft. The unit worked well, and he was quite proud of it. One innovation he had in his unit was to close the sickle drive opening behind the sickle bar. The units in the field always had a problem with grain stubble and other debris clogging the opening and getting debris under the swath, forming canvas drapers. He designed and built a novel sliding closure mechanism to avoid this problem.

Picking rocks was always a springtime chore, and in the earlier years, we used a hay wagon with sideboards on it so it could carry a substantial load of rocks. In our younger years, a team of horses pulled the wagon; we set them on a course down the field, and all kids old enough to pick rocks up and carry them to the wagon were on the crew. We could do approximately fifty-foot swaths on each side of the wagon up and down the field. We had trained the horses to start and stop with verbal commands from Dad or Eddie. During the first few years we owned the Altman farm, some trips down the field resulted in a full wagonload after only one trip across—the field was about 0.4 miles long. When the wagon was full, the horses had to strain pretty hard to pull the load. Mary Jane liked to do that on the field furthest to the south as we would always drink water from the spring because it was the best tasting on our farm. It was always clear and cold.

There were a lot of rocks on the fields at the Altman farm, which later became Eddie's farm. For several years, there was a rock on one field above the spring in the pasture that was pretty solid and always caused the sickle bar on the mower or the cutter bar on the swather to jump, as it stuck out of the ground about four or five inches. One fall, several of us boys were doing fieldwork in that area, and we decided that it was time for that rock to come out of the field. We had shovels and started to dig along one side. After a considerable effort, we finally got to the side of the rock and started digging down. We were down about three or four feet when Dad came along to see how we were doing. He, too, was surprised at the size of the rock. After discussing the situation, we decided to leave the rock in place with the hole as it was. Dad said he would bring home some dynamite, and we would blow the rock out of the ground and break the rock into pieces. Well, ten sticks of dynamite did a good job of bringing the rock out of the ground, but now we had a rock about four feet tall and six feet across. It was some type of granite composition and very sound.

After further discussion, Dad said he would bring some stronger dynamite and a larger amount to break the rock into pieces. He did that—fourteen sticks of 60% dynamite packed in mud did a good job of breaking the rock into smaller, more easily-handled rocks. Eddie and I ended up hauling the pieces of rock to our deposition spot—we were filling a wash to keep it from eroding the waterway further. We used a four-wheel trailer equipped with planks to create a wagon box and ended up with four very heavy loads. A few days later, we were driving along the road and saw a chunk of rock about a half-foot in size in the field about 300 yards from the blast site. We chuckled that it was a good thing that the rock was not close to any buildings as it could have done some damage if pieces had hit one.

Over the years, a lot of nails and other steel debris had accumulated in the farmyard—as a result, we had a lot of flat tires. Grandpa dug out a bunch of v-shaped iron bar magnets from old cars and other engines. He attached eight to ten of them to a 1x4, added small wheels and a handle, and then we had a nail sweeper. We would cover the entire yard surface. During the first few years, we would get a gallon can full of them. Harold or I usually ended up doing the sweeping, as we were old enough and could push the sweeper around pretty well. After four to five years of doing this, the number of nails dwindled to almost nothing, and we finally quit nail sweeping.

Dad was a good steward of the land, but he could have done better. I say that because he switched to a disc plow in the late 1940s because he found out he could better control the amount of turn-over in the land. He prided himself that there was always some stubble showing in the plowed fields so it would catch and hold as much snow as possible while the moldboard plow caused the stubble to turn under. In the 1950s, Freeport Implement had a sub-soiler for a demonstration to help break up the hardpan under the plowed soil. Once Dad used it and saw the positive crop yield results, he bought it and used it on all the fields in a rotation until they switched to the chisel plows in the 1960s. He always practiced crop rotation and made sure the alfalfa rotation reached every field. However, he followed the straight-row edict instead of doing contour farming. Many times, I wondered how to keep the soil on top of the hills instead of accumulating at the bottom of the hills or into the creek. As I worked in fields in my engineering career, I saw a lot of good contour fields, many with terraces, and how well that practice saves the topsoil.

Dad got interested in flying and took lessons after the war. In 1946, he bought an airplane. It was an Aerocoupe, two-passenger, low-wing plane. Dad went all the way with it and constructed a 3/8-mile airstrip through the field across the railroad tracks. He built marker cones to mark it. He also had a windsock at the southwest corner of the shop. The airstrip was officially recognized by the Minnesota aeronautics department. The airstrip later became the field road that is still in place. Earlier, I described how Dad lost his eye in 1947. The Minnesota Aeronautics Division would not grant him an exception to get his private license. That was difficult for him—he used to get the airplane out, taxi it to the runway, speed back and forth on the runway, but never get airborne. It was with sadness that he sold the plane around 1957.

*Shop with the Aerocoupe in front of it—at the southwest most point of the yard buildings. It is approximately fifty feet north of the railroad tracks.*

*Showing off machinery and airplanes in approximately 1953.*

# Chapter 12

# The Sawmill

*Sawmill crew in 1908. Left to right: Nick Hagen, Hubert Moon, Henry Job, George Job, Lewis Job, John Moon, Conrad Job.*

Grandpa built the sawmill on our home farm in 1905; it was in an area to the east of the house in what is now the garden. He started with a circular saw but did not like that it turned 0.35 inches of wood from every cut into sawdust. So, in 1908, he had five-foot diameter wheels cast at the foundry in St. Cloud and built a band mill that used approximately twenty-eight feet of eight-inch band blade. A steam engine powered it. There was also a well close by as it took a lot of water to keep a steam engine running. It also took a lot of wood to heat the water to steam, and the slabs from the sawmill provided most of the fuel to run the steam engine. The sawmill ran from 1905 to 1985, except for a few years in the 1950s where it was not run.

The original sawmill had two bearings holding a 2.5-inch diameter shaft with the wheels cantilevered over the head end. Somewhere in the early years, the upper shaft failed. This caused the upper wheel to fall onto the lower wheel, which broke both. We changed the structure to a three-bearing unit with the third bearing being on the front end of the wheel; the shaft was also changed to a three-inch diameter. This also required a third set of timbers to support the outer bearing. One problem with this three-bearing unit was that it was harder to align the top wheel with the bottom wheel. When this happened, the saw blade would not stay in position on the wheels. This required some precision millwork to get the wheels re-aligned. In about 1948, Dad had Timken tapered roller bearings installed in the upper wheel. This allowed the shaft to remain stationary, and the wheel rotated on the bearings in the center hub. This solved the wheel alignment problem and also required a little less power to run the mill. Dad joked that now, a fly on one side of the wheel would cause it to turn. That design/structure ran successfully until 1957 when Dad and George Beuning rebuilt the mill structure to a steel frame. The new mill frame used the same bearing in that top wheel. We believe that no one was seriously injured while working at the mill during all those years. Safety is a conscious process where you think of it in all the things you do.

*The sawmill from the backside after the rebuild in 1958. Note the simple-open structure compared to the early wood timbers. Sonny is the sawyer.*

The closest thing to a serious injury we had was in 1970 when Dad cut the tips off three of his fingers on the cut-off saw. He said it took him six months to figure out how he did it, as he thought the saw was well guarded. It turns out that the guard on this saw covered the saw blade and used its own weight to hold it down. The guard always contacted the piece of wood before the saw blade did. After his accident, he watched other people operate the saw and observed that when the operator made the cut, they would let go of the handle and grab the piece of wood to move it into position for the next cut. When the operator let go of the handle—the saw is designed for a vertical down-cut with the drive motor as the counterbalance for the saw head—it would return to the "up-stored" position. When it reached the stop position, the saw guard would sometimes bounce and raise from the saw head. When this occurred, the tips of the saw teeth were exposed. On the day he cut his fingers off, he had a particularly large knot, and his hand had grabbed the closest point— the knot which was also very close to the saw teeth —thereby cutting his fingers. He added a spring to stop this from happening.

In 1947, Dad had steel I-beam frames fabricated in the shop at Freeport Implement to replace the 4x6 wood timbers for the sawmill track and carriage base. The track for the carriage was sixty feet long, consisting of two 30-foot sections bolted together. The carriage frame was twenty-four feet long. I often wondered how he got those assemblies home from Freeport; large tractor trailer rigs were not available then. The new track and carriage frame was six inches wider than the old—going from thirty-six inches wide to forty-two inches wide—to better carry the large logs. In the winter, he poured concrete supports installed for the new track frame. All the installation—assembly and testing for accuracy of the lumber—was done in the winter, so he was ready for the spring sawing season.

*The front end of the mill in 1947 with the steel carriage frame and track. Dad is at the sawyer position. The box at an incline to the right of the carriage is the sawdust elevator.*

Grandpa tells of the time in the early days when a steam engine tractor powered the sawmill. Since those tractors were not very maneuverable once set up for sawing, we left them in position for extended periods. The drive used a six–inch–wide flat belt. To keep the drive belt from stretching too much, he devised a simple idler tensioning device which rode on the slack side (top) of the belt. The crew could raise a lever and unload it via a vertical idler pulley that operated in a slide when the mill was not running. To assure they had adequate tension and to keep the belt from slipping, he placed a rock in the box on the top side of the idler. One day while sawing, the log pinched the saw blade and stopped it. The action was so fast that the slack side of the belt tightened and threw the weight box and the rock up. The weight box had a top stop with the rock loose in the box. The rock catapulted through the roof of the mill and came down outside the mill. Needless to say, we retained the rock in the weight box after that.

The cutting blade on the sawmill was a band blade with cutting teeth on the front edge. The lower wheel on the sawmill was below-ground in a pit, while the upper wheel was in a large timber frame. There were covers over the front of both the lower wheels so that the sawdust would drop into an elevator, which would carry the sawdust away from the mill and the upper wheel to reduce the amount of sawdust flying from the blade. There was a secondary reason for the upper cover: one time while sawing, a piece broke loose from a log while the carriage was being returned for the next cut. This piece of wood hooked the back of the saw blade and pushed it from the wheels. The blade cut a neat groove into both the upper and lower covers. The covers being in place kept the blade from flying freely, protecting the sawyer—my dad.

Many years, we sawed so much wood that we had to shovel the sawdust, so there could be room for the elevator to bring out the fresh sawdust—the point where the elevator discharged the sawdust onto the pile was approximately ten feet above the ground. Once the younger kids were old enough, it was our job to shovel the sawdust away from the elevator so there was room for more sawdust to fall onto the pile. In a picture of Ed on the carriage with the largest log we cut, you can see part of the sawdust pile behind him. Art tells of times when, with a strong west or northwest wind, the sawdust would reach the driveway.

*The largest log we cut—approximately 54 in. in diameter. We had to cut off a large knot in order to get it through the mill; we also had to take off the upper guide until it was fully slabbed. Dad is at the right end of the log and Eddie is on the carriage. Note the sawdust pile behind the carriage. It had been a windy spring and the pile was quite long.*

When cutting, the sawmill had a very distinctive, high-pitch whine. You could hear the difference between softwood and a hardwood log by the sound. You could also tell when the saw cut a nail or something other than wood; it was usually a very sharp zing, and then the boards would have a mark on them where the damaged teeth did not cut the same way the rest of the teeth did. The original

Twin-City Model KT grey tractor, the predecessor to the Minneapolis-Moline Company, drove the mill.

Until about 1952 or 1953, the wheels on the mill were approximately six inches wide; the new blades purchased were eight inches wide. We could use these blades until they were approximately 5.5 inches wide—at that point, it became difficult to keep the blade running properly on the wheels. In that time frame, Dad had rings cast, and the wheels and the rings machined to make the wheels eight inches wide, allowing new blades to be ten inches wide. This allowed hundreds of additional hours of usage per blade.

The teeth on the saw had a swage to them which made the tooth tip approximately 0.125 inches wide while the blade was 0.059 inches thick. This allowed the blade to run with little friction through the space behind the cut. Normal operation would allow a sharp blade to cut lumber all day. If we cut a lot of hardwood in a day—oak, ash, etc.—we had to install a sharp blade early in the afternoon to keep the mill operating efficiently. If you were away from the mill, you could tell how large a log was or how hard the wood was based on how much the speed of the tractor engine decreased. I can remember many large hardwood logs pulled the tractor engine speed down to almost half normal operation, and then the carriage could be returned and the log set for the next cut before the engine had fully recovered.

*The front end of the sawmill in early 1944. Note the large slab pile to the left—the tractor powering it is the 1936 Twin City "KT". It also has the original wooded track and carriage frame. It looks like Grandpa is the sawyer.*

In the years after 1945, the local farmers had a lot of timber capable of making dimensional lumber for building repair and construction; there were no longer restrictions on money one could spend on construction, either. Many of the logs that were delivered to our yard were of substantial size—eighteen to twenty-four inches in diameter. When loading these large logs on the carriage, the crew had to be careful as the carriage was almost thrown off the track several times. Additionally, the wood beams from the track and carriage were starting to rot. Therefore, Dad decided to replace the wooden track and carriage frame with steel I-beams. When he designed the replacement track and carriage, he changed the track from thirty-six inches wide to forty-two inches wide. This was a very successful improvement as the larger logs could be handled without concern.

In the 1940s and 1950s, it was not unusual to have the yard full of logs in the spring or the fall. During the early 1940s—the World War II years—lumber was almost impossible to get. A lot of our sawmill business was due to that demand. During those years, there was no dimensional lumber available—1x4s, 1x6s, 2x4s, 2x6s, etc.—but timbers were. People would purchase the timbers and bring them to us, and Dad would recut them to dimensional lumber for their use. That added quite a bit of additional sawing work.

*Pile of logs in yard. In the 1940s and early 1950s, there were often three piles deep across the yard.*

We operated the mill without the slab cut-off—where the slabs were cut into firewood lengths immediately after they came off the logs until about 1948. One person carried the finished lumber into one pile while another carried the slabs into another pile. By the end of the spring and fall cutting season, there was always a very substantial pile of slabs to cut into firewood. We did this on a bench-type bucksaw. That was not very efficient as it required us to carry many slabs a long way to cut them. Dad mounted a bucksaw on the front of the tractor to make the cutting job easier; the first version was on the original Twin Cities model KT tractor. We could move it as necessary to a position close to the slab pile, so there was not as much time wasted waiting for the slabs. After we cut the slabs, we threw the cut pieces into a hay wagon with special plank sides, so the trailer could hold more. We had to unload the firewood into a pile from which we moved it to the house or loaded it again to sell. I can remember many years when the upper yard between the house and the railroad tracks had a woodpile covering several hundred feet in length and ten to twelve feet high.

Once while sawing the bearing next to the drive pulley on the lower drive, the shaft started to smoke. They quickly shut down the mill. Investigation showed that the bearing had gotten hot and the Babbitt (the bearing material) had melted from the bearing. Evidently, oil was not getting to the bearing surface, therefore preventing proper operation. After it had cooled off, Dad and Grandpa disassembled the bearing and removed it from the shaft. They carefully cleaned any remaining Babbitt and other material from the bearing housing. They also cleaned and polished the shaft in the bearing area because any imperfections could cause a future failure. Then they replaced the lower bearing housing half in its location, positioned the upper bearing housing half, and bolted it in place. Next, they checked the bearing location on the shaft and were satisfied that the bearing housing was centered on the shaft. Then, they placed a thin piece of sheet metal where the bearing housing halves met—there had to be a hole (called a sprue) for the liquid Babbitt to run from the upper half of the bearing to the lower half. They sealed the ends of the bearing housing at the shaft so the liquid Babbitt would be retained in the housing.

With everything in place, and the bearing housings bolted securely, they poured hot, melted Babbitt into the bearing housing until it was full. After it cooled completely, they unbolted the bearing and carefully cut through the sprue, the Babbitt connecting the upper and lower halves. To ensure the Babbitt material had not adhered to the shaft, they rotated the shaft at the wheel. Then they removed the bearing from the shaft. They had to carefully cut oil grooves into the Babbitt so oil could flow from the top center of the bearing and lubricate the entire bearing. Then they could reassemble the bearing on the shaft and check that the shaft with the wheel and drive pulley were in place and properly lubricated so it would rotate freely. Then the repair was complete.

These bearings each had an "oil cup" above them that allowed oil to drip into the bearing, thereby lubricating the bearing assemblies. We had to fill each cup at least once per day, sometimes twice. There were no oil seals on these shafts, so any excess oil ran to the edge of the bearing where it mixed with sawdust, creating a wet oil ring around the edge—in a sense, creating a seal and keeping out other dirt. When studying lubrication theory in school, I found that the oil film between the bearing and the shaft carried the load of the shaft in the bearing.

In Minnesota, the ground would freeze during the winters. In the spring, while the ground was thawing, there were usually a few days when we could not operate the mill because the mainframe and the carriage supports would move, and the boards would cut in a parallelogram shape. The boards would also not be straight as the carriage supports in the ground would move and cause the track for the carriage to be crooked, resulting in saw cuts that were not straight.

When the outer surface of the log had dirt on it, or there were nails or other things in the logs, we had to replace the blade immediately. Other things we ran into over the years were fences and even a horseshoe in the middle of a log; the father of the owner of the logs said, "One of the kids must have done that." Cutting into the horseshoe did less damage than some nails. Sometimes the damage was very minor, then they would continue to run, but there was almost always a tell-tale line on the board from where the teeth were damaged. Depending on how much damage was done to the teeth, the saw blade would have to be re-swaged to get it to cut properly. We had to re-swage all the teeth on the blade, re-shape all the teeth, and then re-grind the teeth to make the blade fully functional. If the blade damage was severe, it would require the swaging and shaping operation to go twice around the blade to get the teeth consistent.

Many times, Dad worked three to four hours on a blade to return it to a fully functional state; this time was usually in the evening and into the night to have a sharp blade ready for the next day. Sometimes the damage was not worked out until the second swaging round. The blade was functional, but the surface of the lumber had lines from the imperfection. Until we built the shop in 1947, all the tools were in the basement of the house, and Dad did the saw sharpening there. There were many evenings when Dad was shaping the teeth and running the saw blade through the grinder to have saw blades ready to use for the next day's operation. The grinding operation was quite noisy, so it was noisy upstairs in the house. The grinding operation consisted of the grinder wheel coming down into the recess of the tooth, sharpening the front edge of the tooth. Then, while a cam on the grinder arm would raise the grinding wheel, another cam moved the saw blade forward and sharpened the top side of the tooth.

Dad had a hammering table and some special hammers with which he tried to hammer out some wrinkles or other deficiencies that worked into the saw blades through use. The table was approximately 16x30x3 inches of cast iron, which served as an anvil, so it had sufficient mass to allow the hammer to work the material of the blade. Dad always complained that he did not have the expertise to properly do this hammering job. In the late 1950s or early 60s, he met Arnold Campbell—who worked in a commercial sawmill in Northern Minnesota—who did that work; he taught Dad how to do it. When the blades were damaged beyond Dad's skill level, he sent them to a saw repair shop in St. Paul for repair.

Sometimes, a saw blade would develop a crack, usually in the back edge. Dad would center punch the blade to the deepest part of the crack in the blade. This usually stopped the crack from propagating further into the blade. They would weld the cracks and grind the surface smooth. Those welds usually held until the blade was worn out, but I can remember taking some blades out of service because they had too many cracks or the cracks became too long. Dad would not use a blade if it would likely fail.

Another interesting incident occurred when Dad was sawing. A piece of wood broke off the bottom side of a log, and a sharp edge dropped in the lower saw guide—the guide is one hardwood block, usually hard maple, on each side of the blade to retain it so it will cut straight. If left in place, the piece of wood could get hot enough to start a fire. My dad saw it and hollered and motioned to my brother—who was on the backside of the mill in the scaler position—to push it out with a pointed stick kept for that purpose. There happened to be a man visiting the operation who was standing behind my Dad and watching. Not thinking, he started to reach to the saw blade from the front-cutting tooth side to pick out the piece of wood with his hand. Luckily, another member of our crew happened to be in the area and saw the man start to reach towards the saw blade; he grabbed the man by the back of his collar and jerked him back. My dad showed the man his temper that day and almost bodily threw him off our place.

When the kids were old enough, and school was not in session, we became part of the sawing crew. At first, it was Dolores on the carriage and then Dorothy and Eddie. As we boys grew older, we replaced the girls on the crew. Dorothy became particularly adept at the scaling position, and she was the preferred person for that position as she could figure the number of board feet per log and add up the total number of board feet per page on the ledger. That saved Dad a lot of time in the evening, as he always had his saw ledger up to date for the next day's work. All the girls were part of the saw crew at times; Clara and Ethel were somewhat exceptions to this, as they spent little time working the sawmill.

*Dolores and Dorothy in the scaler position, working the back end of the mill. This would have been prior to 1945 when there was a shortage of men to fill those jobs. Note: this customer is loading his lumber on a trailer to take home.*

Operating the carriage was a very important job on the mill, and it was very risky. Normally, the carriage operator had to pull out the dogs—these teeth locked the log in place while the blade did the cutting. The operator pulled them from headblocks two and three (the rails where the log slid on during the sawing process) while the log was being turned and then reset them for the next position. Then he positioned the headblocks for the next cut; it involved a lot of moving the headblocks back and forth during the log positioning for the sawing process. Lastly, when the cut was done, he engaged the offset lever to move the log cut surface away from the saw blade to avoid drag and potential problems. The reverse direction speed was approximately twice that of the fastest forward speed. This became risky if there was some bark or if a sliver of the log came loose during the reverse action. If the carriage was not stopped, it could pull the saw blade off the wheels and cause damage. The stops for these situations were usually very abrupt, and if one was not paying attention, the momentum could throw you off the carriage. Most of us who operated the carriage were dumped off at least once. I do not remember it happening to me, although there were several occasions when I was hanging on to the actuator lever for dear life. Art says he has the same record, but he knew you had to hold on to keep from getting dumped.

The scaler had to record the size and number of boards from each log. In addition, Dad appreciated if you learned to figure the board feet from each log while doing all the work of that position. I got so I could also figure the total number of board feet on each page as I worked. As I got older, I did it when I worked the scaler position.

At various times, we got a report on how much wood we cut in a given year. In the 1940s and 1950s, it was not unusual to cut over 100,000 board feet of lumber in a year. On a good day, we could cut 5000 board feet per day. You can do the math as to how many days of sawing we did a year.

One spring, as it got warmer, we started having bumblebees flying around the scaler and lumber handler positions. It took about two days to figure out they had a nest in the sawdust where the lumber roll started. When we dropped large boards on the lumber roll or the ground for re-sawing, it disturbed the bees. I believe we used oil drained from engines to kill them in the nest. If "Raid" existed at that time, we did not have any.

Elm trees made very good dimensional lumber. Some of the barns we built had red elm 2x10 floor joists. However, there was a white elm version of that tree, commonly called piss elm, that you did not want to make into dimensional lumber if it wasn't fully dry. If the trees were not dry when sawed, the lumber would curl and be worthless. One time, a person brought a good number of logs for us to cut into 2x4s and 2x6s. Included in the group were some very good-looking piss elm logs, and he wanted 2x4s from them. Dad told him the studs cut from those logs would not work well; they would not be straight. The customer, being always right, insisted on having the logs marked for 2x4s cut into them. Dad obliged him—he got a pile of scrap lumber because every one of the 2x4s from those logs curled, so they were unusable.

I would be remiss if I did not include the help that Grandpa was over the years, in the summers before 1948 and after they came back from California. When they were on the farm during the summers and after he had recuperated, Grandpa took over the sawyer role many days. Into his 70's, he could still do that job very well. He needed help on turning the larger logs during the slabbing cut process. Other than that, he did that job very well, and I believe he enjoyed it.

*Sawmill crew in 1984. Left to right: Jerry Pfau, Dad, Loren Beutz, Sonny, Eddie*

*Sawmill crew in 1984. Left to right: Augie Wohletz, Carl Schultzenberg, Roger, Sonny, Eddie, Ralph, Jerry Pfau. Photo taken from the backside of the sawmill. Note the edger on the right, which was built by Dad and added in the 1960's.*

On the last day we used the sawmill, Cliff and his family took videos of the operation—from it, you can get a pretty good idea of what it was like to be part of the mill operation. In 1997, when Dad was in his 80s, the amount of lumber cut had substantially dropped off. Dad asked about keeping the mill running. While Louis was somewhat agreeable, he was more interested in what the next generation wanted to do. David had no interest in learning the sawyer role or keeping the mill in operation. Dad sold the mill to the Albany Pioneer Park where it resides today.

# Hunting

There were always guns in the house—on the mantle above the bureau and in cabinets on the south side of the dining room. The most used gun was a .22 caliber Savage octagonal barrel pump action rifle. There was also a Fox 12-gauge double-barrel shotgun and the "Long Tom" 12-gauge single shot shotgun. Later, we also had a single-shot .22 caliber rifle. Dad had a Smith & Weston .22 caliber six-shot revolver, but it was always put away. There was also a .32 caliber snub-nosed revolver, but there did not seem to be any ammunition for it. In the later years, we also had another single-shot 12-gauge shotgun.

The .22 savage rifle was the gun with which all of us learned to shoot. Dad got it when he was a boy. Over the years, it shot many shell cartons. A carton consisted of ten boxes of fifty shells each. The rifle was so well-used that in the mid-1950s, sometimes the brass cartridge case would break at the rim, and it would not always eject the spent cartridge. The barrel was worn where the cartridge seated for firing, and the ejection mechanism was worn, so it would not properly grasp the edge of the casing for ejection. Dad had a friend—who built and refurbished guns as a hobby—rebuild the barrel and ejection mechanism so that it worked properly. It is still a functional gun. This rifle was very accurate in that you could clamp the barrel in a vise, and it would exactly shoot one bullet on top of another at approximately fifteen feet. Dad was a very good shot with this gun. More than once, he demonstrated that he could shoot a spent .22 short casing from inside a fence staple-free hand at ten paces.

One time, they had a rooster who had reached butchering age. The problem was that no one could catch it with a poultry hook. Dad waited on him one day and shot him through the head. The rooster was then butchered and eaten. One year, we had picked all the Duchess apples except for one, which was out on a limb out of reach. Dad got it down by shooting off the stem where it attached to the tree.

Grandpa loved to hunt. He had a good selection of guns during the years he farmed because he hunted deer and other large animals. When they came back to live with us in 1950, he had only a Fox 12-gauge double-barrel shotgun. What happened to his other guns is unknown. He was most fond of hunting ducks, and after they came to live with us—and he was well enough—he was planning the start of the waterfowl hunting season in mid-September. The hunting season always started at noon on a Saturday in mid-September, and everyone was in place so the shooting could start at noon. In the mid-1950s, he and Art also did some deer hunting with shotguns and slugs. There was a tin target set up in the field to the south of the tracks for practice. When the shot hit the tin target, it sounded like heavy hail on a tin roof.

Grandpa once bought a prize hunting dog and brought him home. To keep him from running off until he adjusted to his new home, Grandpa tied him up close to the back door of the house. Something caught the dog's attention, and he got excited and jumped over the guard rail on the side of the steps. Grandpa found him hanging after he was already dead. Grandpa was quite upset with himself over it.

In the early 1950s, we built a hunting boat out of one-inch basswood boards appropriately reinforced and sealed. It was a yearly event to get the hunting boat out a week or so before the start of the season. We would fill it with water so it would swell and seal up all the cracks—that way, the boat would be watertight. We usually had to fill it several times to get the boat leak-tight. Once the wood had swelled up, we kept it in water—usually in the slough to the southeast of our farm, referred to as Friedel's Lake, and it would stay watertight. The boat was still serviceable in 1960.

After the hunting season had started, one of us boys would slip away from morning chores, grab a shotgun, and hike down to a few slough holes where we knew the ducks liked to hang out. Often, we came back with a few ducks to add to our meals.

One year, while still very young, Harold and I went hunting with Lawrence Wensmann. Harold had the .22 savage, and Lawrence had their bolt action .22. I wanted to find out how to set the safety on Lawrence's rifle, and Lawrence proceeded to show me how to do it. When I tried, I forgot to hold the firing pin bolt when pulling the trigger, so the gun fired. Dad had trained us to always point the gun down when not sighting or shooting at something. We were fortunate in that I had pointed the rifle at the ground. As it turned out, the muzzle was still only several inches from Lawrence's foot.

I remember we got a BB gun to learn to shoot. Harold and I carried that for several years when we went hunting with Grandpa and the bigger brothers. One fall, while on the Friedel side of the fence at the swamp, a duck flew by close enough for me to try to shoot it with the BB gun. I missed, of course, but I distinctly saw the pellet fly from the gun past the duck. It made me understand better Grandpa's lecture on leading the flying object and projectile trajectory.

It was not unusual for several of us to hunt on Saturday and Sunday afternoons. We would usually walk to the slough behind the house and walk around it. If the hunting boat was at the lake, one of us would take the boat, and the rest would walk around the lake to chase up ducks.

One fall, I was the only boy left at home, and I went out hunting pheasants as usual. Our dog Sport—who was a very good hunting dog—and I chased a pheasant on the west side of the lake. The pheasant flew to the southwest corner of the lake. We proceeded to that corner, and Sport chased the pheasant again as we got to the area where he landed, but we were too far away for a good shot. It landed again on the east side of the lake. On around the lake Sport and I went. Sport again picked up his track and flushed him up. I got off a shot, but the distance and angle were bad. I missed, so the pheasant flew across to the west side of the lake. Sport and I dutifully hiked around the lake, and on the west side where the pheasant landed, Sport again picked up the track. This time, when the pheasant was flushed up, I was ready for it and bagged it. This was in a period of years in the late 1950s when the pheasant population was very low. I felt that one bird was a successful hunt.

I believe 1951 was a very dry year, and there was almost no water in Friedel's lake. Art and Sonny made mud shoes. They were pieces of one-inch board about twelve inches wide by fifteen to eighteen inches long. They had a leather strap nailed to them so they could fasten them to the shoes—a crude version of snowshoes for mud. In these shoes, they walked around the mudflats of the lake. I don't remember that they got any game, but they had a good time walking around in the middle of the lake.

# Chapter 14

# Conclusion

I cannot close without passing on this rather humorous story is of a local carpenter, Pete, and plumber, Elmo, who were having a beer at one of the local taverns when Elmo came up with a 10-penny nail from his pocket. He reached over and dropped the nail into Pete's bottle of beer and said, "Pete, I spiked your beer." They got busy talking, and Pete switched the beer bottles. The next swig Elmo took, he swallowed the nail. Several X-rays and some days later, the nail passed through his system. Needless to say, Elmo was lucky. The incident made the local paper at the time.

One thing not specifically mentioned anywhere else is that Dad was twenty when he started farming and was twenty-one when he and Ma—who was twenty-three at the time—were married. While he sired and raised a large family, his accomplishments in improving and rebuilding the farmstead and sawmill are quite impressive. Equally impressive was Ma's contribution to this endeavor. She kept us fed, clothed, and educated through all our childhood years.

The family members are now aged; my oldest living sister turned ninety this year. There are now seven of the original eleven left, and all of us are over seventy-five. The family saw sixty-four grandchildren, and I am not able to count the great-grandchildren as I have lost track. Eight of the original children were farmers, and numerous nieces and nephews are in the profession, so our up-bringing rubbed off well.

All our family members are practicing Catholics as we were raised. This speaks volumes for how we were raised, and I think it is a tribute to our parents.

The farm is operated by my nephew as a dairy farm. He has increased the number of milk cows milked so he can make a decent living. By increasing the number of cows, he has had to increase the size of his barn and add hay storage. My brother Sonny and he purchased more land a number of years ago, so he has a larger acreage base to work. The house we grew up in was torn down, another house was put in its place. Included in that is a remote heating system, with the hot water pumped into the house as needed. I believe my nephew still heats with wood but in a special boiler unit that is very efficient. The smoke house was also torn down a number of years ago.

The Friedel farm was sold to the National Wildlife Federation as a wildlife refuge and is exactly that. All the buildings were torn down, and there are now abundant deer, wild turkeys and other wildlife, and no acres are tilled. It is a little unusual for me to see trees and brush where there used to be a productive field.

Writing this manuscript has been an interesting experience and I had to research many details I never knew before. I, like many writers, kept wanting to make it more inclusive, but finally said that this has to be it. It was fun and I hope the family appreciates it.

# Acknowledgments

I would be remiss if I did not acknowledge my brothers and sisters who contributed a lot of information for this endeavor and helped me get the facts as close to correct as we knew. They are Dolores, Dorothy, Ed, Art, Louis, Mary Jane, Clara, and Ethel. Also, Roger and Carol Job made a special effort to find some pictures that I used. In addition, Jessie Storlien—archivist at the Stearns History Museum in St. Cloud, MN—was an invaluable resource on some of the property information on Andreas's homestead. Lastly, I want to thank my nieces and nephews who kept pestering me to get this job done so they could enjoy it.

www.ingramcontent.com/pod-product-compliance
Lightning Source LLC
Chambersburg PA
CBHW071329150726
47997CB00002B/649